We live in a culture filled with comp
are held in high value in the lives of
not exclude Christian women. As a
social stratifications, both in small

need for women of all ages to be exposed to this book. *Dethroning the Queen* by Alicia Sheppard is a timely book that will meet women face to face in their own experiences, expose them to biblical principles, and empower them to overcome the unnecessary weights that flaw and hinder their personal relationships with other women. Experience the freedom to have whole and healthy relationships as sisters in the body of Christ. Let's allow *Dethroning the Queen* to provide a change in our culture that will Crown the Princess in all of us.

DORETHA O'QUINN, PH.D., MINISTER, PROFESSOR AND AUTHOR

Wow! What a timely and anointed message to women globally. Alicia communicates the heart of God for His girls and exposes ploys the enemy has used for centuries to prevent women in the body of Christ from experiencing true friendships and fulfillment in life and ministry. This is a message of freedom!

LAURIE ENGQUIST, WORSHIP LEADER, SPEAKER & ASSOC.
PASTOR OF PRAISE CITY CHURCH IN AZ

Alicia Sheppard so succinctly pinpoints the pollutants that hinder our souls from prospering. Her analogy of the bee sting creatively brings relevance to her pungent realities. In the same way all stings swell, so do these negative characteristics grow in our hearts if left unattended. This book inspires and equips the reader to "kill" the bee, strengthen our personal identity, and celebrate the uniqueness of others.

DEVI TITUS
FOUNDER/CEO THE MENTORING MANSION, SPEAKER, AUTHOR

Praise God for the accuracy of the truths revealed in this book! Alicia Sheppard has created a road map to understanding where the division between women lies. *Dethroning the Queen* has cutting, cultivating, and in-depth detail that gets to the heart of the matter and promotes healing within relationships. It will influence all areas of your life—a must have.

ARIYAN JOHNSON MCDANIEL
ACTRESS, CHOREOGRAPHER, ARTISTIC DIRECTOR
FAITHFUL CENTRAL BIBLE CHURCH

Alicia Renee Sheppard

Dethroning the Queen

Getting Rid of Rivalry and Resentment

VMI PUBLISHERS
SISTERS, OREGON

Published by
VMI PUBLISHERS
Sisters, Oregon
www.vmipublishers.com

ISBN: 1-933204-57-5
ISBN 13: 978-1-933204-57-4
Library of Congress Control Number:
Printed in the USA

Cover design by Kara M. Elsberry

CONTENTS

Introduction: Queen Bees

"Let us throw off everything that hinders and the sin that so easily entangles, and let us run with perseverance the race marked out for us."
HEBREWS 12:1

WHAT, OR RATHER, WHO is a "Queen Bee"? I'm not talking about the ones that produce honey, but I am talking about a kind that stings. I am afraid, though, that these Queen Bees aren't insects. They're women. They are the ones we encounter in elementary school, middle school, and high school. We see them at work, in the mall, at social gatherings, and even in churches or Bible study groups. They are on television as reality TV show personalities. Where there's a crowd, there's sure to be at least one or two Queens in the bunch. All of us can point them out when we come across them—and most of us have probably been stung by one.

What do people mean when they refer to a woman as a "Queen Bee"? There tends to be a specific type that is labeled this way. She's the leader of the clique, the girl you love to hate. She's mean, she's superior, and she's better than everyone else. Everyone hates her, and everyone wants to be her. Often she is seen as being mean, bossy, or self-centered, while at the same time being somehow fabulous and powerful, too. She is Regina George in the movie *Mean Girls*[1] (a film I personally believe portrays the Queen Bee phenomenon excellently!).

Most of us have personal examples. What type of woman makes the words "Queen Bee" come to your mind? I think of Mimi Johnson, the

Dethroning the Queen

popular girl in middle school, rallying the other kids in a class-wide plot to drench me with super soakers and water balloons on the last day of school. I think of the ruling female clique singing out during recess, "Tick-Tock, the game is LOCKED, you should have been here at 8 o'clock!" when less popular girls walked up to join the double-dutch games. I think of my best friend yelling out in front of the entire class (when I walked up to school late one day), "Maybe she was trying to get some breast implants!" (I was a very "flat-chested" fifth-grader).

I've heard women talk about all kinds of Queen Bee experiences. Perhaps you've attended a social event and felt the icy chill of other women's unanimous and automatic disapproval of you. Or maybe a cheerful greeting from you was met with a sideways glance and a wimpy hello that felt more like, "I hate you!" Maybe you've seen the pursed lips, the rolled eyes, or felt you were the object of the muffled laughs and whispers in the corner. Or worse yet, maybe you've had the sneaking suspicion you've been the object of the group's discussion after a roomful of chatter immediately stopped when you walked through the door. Have you ever been scared to dress up when going to a new church? I know I have. Why? Because you're afraid some of the women might take one look at your makeup and earrings and cry, "Jezebel!" Maybe you hate talking to your girlfriends about your husband or the men you like because you're afraid they'll vie for their attention. And maybe you've had so many negative encounters with Queen Bees that you've thrown up your hands in despair and thought, "I just don't like women!"

Yes, sadly, most of us can recount times when we've felt abused by a Queen Bee. For many women, female-female relationships are wars. They become associated with hurtfulness, meanness, pain, and distrust. More and more women's lives paint a picture of broken friendships and bitter enemies—and much of this is because of various encounters with Queen Bees.

Queen Bees

The Other Side of the Story

Now let's consider the flip side. Sometimes the Queen Bee is not another woman. Sometimes we're the Queen Bees.

Though it's sad to admit this, if the truth be told, I can think of times when I was on the other side of the Queen Bee equation—punishing a girl I was angry with by talking about her to one of her friends (in hopes of getting the friend on my side), secretly feeling satisfied when an "opponent" felt trumped by my outfit, or glorying in my heart of hearts in the fact that my attributes made certain women (whom I didn't particularly care for) feel inferior. Ouch!

Harsh, isn't it? But it happens! Can we please talk about it? These are things that happen out in the open and beneath the surface. In biting comments, or in the silent secrets of our hearts. In schoolyards. In church pews. Between enemies. Between friends.

So is it her…or is it you? Maybe you're the victim. Or maybe you're the victimizer. The chances are you've probably been both. It happens many ways. Perhaps you've secretly, or openly, flirted with another woman's husband? Spread gossip to sabotage a woman you felt threatened by? Comforted yourself with an adversary's failures? Looked a girl up and down condemningly because in reality you just felt she looked a whole lot cuter than you? The point is, no matter how overt or subtle our attacks against other women may be, it's all part of the same game—and most of us have been players as well as pawns.

Queen Bees Come in Many Forms, Not Just One!

The interesting thing about my personal confession is I always considered myself to be the nice girl! I was never the mean girl type. I never joined in the schoolyard teasing bashes. In fact, I was dubbed "Goody Two Shoes" by my classmates, and referred to as such on an almost daily basis! I was always quick to befriend the "loners," "losers," and laughed-at. And, I had a very severe distaste for mean-spirited, catty, vindictive girls. When it

11

came to Queen Bees, I was the victim, never the victimizer! Or was I?

Over time, the Lord made me very sensitive to this Queen Bee dynamic between women, and in doing so, He gave me understanding about the many different forms Queen Bees can take. That's when I had to admit that I was one, too, but the tricky thing about my kind was that it was accomplishable without so much as a single word. I wasn't the eye-rolling, man-stealing, taunting, teasing, hair-flipping kind. On the contrary, I tend to think I'm rather polite. But the Holy Spirit revealed to me that when I let Queen Bee tendencies rise up in me, I was more like the Silent Stinger. It was my inward satisfaction with other people's discomfort that was the problem. It was my seemingly innocent conversation with Cathy that was really a direct blow against Lisa, whom I knew was sitting nearby within earshot. Most often it had nothing to do with my actions or words, and everything to do with my heart.

Women—some of us are masterfully deceptive when we want to be. We can be in church, head of a ministry, in choir, attending a Bible study, respected by others, and yet wrestling with these issues on the inside, attacking other women in the secret corners of our hearts. As a result, Queen Bees can come in many different forms.

THE ESSENCE OF A QUEEN BEE

We tend to have a certain picture in our minds when we think of a Queen Bee. We usually picture the popular girl—the center of attention who is secretly insecure until everyone else feels like crap. But there are other kinds. Quiet as it's kept, Queen Bees can also be low key, in the background, soft-spoken, or seemingly polite. How? Because ultimately, that Queen Bee mentality is really an inward quality rather than an external one. Ultimately, it has nothing to do with how popular you are, or how mean you are with your words. It's a heart condition that plagues women who are at odds with other women. And that characteristic, that hostility toward other woman, that quality that makes women feel like another woman is an enemy and that drives women into antagonist relationships with one another—that characteristic can be found in all sorts of women. It can be found in the quiet woman sitting in the corner at a social gathering who looks a woman up and down when she walks in the room, itemizing all her flaws and trying to convince herself that she's not as cute as she thinks. It can be the intercessor in a prayer meeting who uses prayer as a time to spill gossip. A Queen Bee can also be a woman who is offended by another woman and refuses to forgive her in her heart. They don't always appear to be like the prom queens, the cheerleaders, the snobby sorority girls, the evil stepsisters, or other Queen Bee stereotypes. No, Queen Bees come in many forms. Realizing that fact is key in reversing the problem.

Redefining a Queen Bee

At the heart of the matter, a Queen Bee is any woman who is sinful or ungodly in her relationships with other women. It's really that simple. It's not a complicated stereotype; it's just sin. You become like a Queen Bee whenever you commit sin that specifically manifests in your relationships with other women. Any sinful attitude or action directed against women is that of a Queen Bee. Queen Bee characteristics are those that create some form of hostility between women. Also, anything that promotes the idea that women are enemies is a Queen Bee characteristic. In this book, we are mainly going to explore ten major Queen Bee characteristics: comparison, competition, jealousy, antipathy, discord, judgment, exclusivity, slander, subtext, and pride. Each of these creates rivalry, division, or hostility between women. The sad thing is, this Queen Bee dynamic happens all the time—even in the kingdom of God.

The Kingdom of God: A Kingdom of Love and Unity

Despite how poorly it seems women sometimes get along, it's certainly not supposed to be that way for the women of God. 1 Corinthians 13:4–8a says, "Love is patient, love is kind. It does not envy, it does not boast, it is not proud. It is not rude, it is not self-seeking, it is not easily angered, it keeps no record of wrongs. Love does not delight in evil but rejoices with the truth. It always protects, always trusts, always hopes, always perseveres. Love never fails."

Do you notice all the wonderful adjectives and concepts used in this passage of Scripture? Patience, kindness, humility, selflessness, forgiveness, rejoicing, protection, trust, hope, and perseverance are all characteristics of godly love and relationships. These are quite different from envy, boasting, pride, rudeness, selfishness, irritability, judgment, cruelty, betrayal, distrust, despair, and failure. Yet, which of the two lists more accurately describes your experience or perception of female relationships? Too often, the answer is the latter. Women of God must realize love is the greatest commandment, and the Queen Bee mentality is contrary to love in every way!

The other important dimension of godly relationships that is contrary to the Queen Bee dynamic is unity. We are called to be one body. Paul emphasizes this point right before he talks about love in 1 Corinthians 12. We will talk about the nature of the body of Christ in more depth in chapter two, but it is important to understand that unity is a huge dimension of godly relationships, and is one of the main qualities that is lacking in many female relationships.

CHANGE IS GOING TO COME!

Well, despite it all, there is good news! God has a plan to unify the women in the kingdom of God. He wants to bring us out of the Queen Bee mentality and into right standing with Him and with each other. In this book, we are going to deal with the issues that create rivalry between the women of God, and women in general. First, we are going to expose the issues. Hebrews 4:13 says, "Nothing in all creation is hidden from God's sight. Everything is uncovered and laid bare before the eyes of him to whom we must give an account." So much of our female issues lie beneath the surface, but God sees it all. Whether we are like Regina in the movie *Mean Girls* or like the quiet woman refusing to forgive others in her heart, God sees the Queen Bee in us! There is no use hiding it, and in order to let Him change us, we must let Him expose those issues to us.

We are also going to let God explain these issues to us. Understanding the issues is key, for God says, "My people are destroyed from lack of knowledge" (Hosea 4:6). Gaining understanding about these issues is a very critical step. Insight is useful for correction, and it will help facilitate healing and deliverance.

Finally, we are going to let the Holy Spirit eradicate these issues with the Word of God. Hebrews 4:12 says, "For the word of God is living and active. Sharper than any double-edged sword, it penetrates even to dividing soul and spirit, joints and marrow; it judges the thoughts and attitudes of the heart." The Word of truth pierces through the gunk in our hearts and cuts away everything that is not like God.

We don't want to be found guilty because we have failed to understand how we are dishonoring God with our faulty relationships with women. We don't want to be hindered in our walks with God because of our struggle with Queen Bee issues. We don't want our relationships to be destroyed from a lack of knowledge. We want to have understanding about these things so we can get rid of them. So we are going to confront these Queen Bee characteristics with the Word of truth and let the gunk be cut away. In other words, we are going to let the Holy Spirit dethrone the Queen!

Prayer

Dear Lord,

Thank You for being a constant friend that I can always trust in. I praise You for Your unfailing love; You are the shoulder I can always lean on. Now Lord, I know it is part of Your plan for me to experience godly relationships, so I invite Your Holy Spirit to start the process of exposing, explaining, and erasing areas of weakness in my relationships with women. Please heal me from the hurt of past experiences with women, and cleanse me from the times I was guilty of sinful attitudes and actions toward women. Gently and lovingly dethrone the Queen in my heart, and begin teaching me how to have true sisterhood. In Jesus' Name, I pray. Amen.

Memory Verse

"Love is patient, love is kind. It does not envy, it does not boast, it is not proud. It is not rude, it is not self-seeking, it is not easily angered, it keeps no record of wrongs. Love does not in delight in evil, but rejoices with the truth. It always protects, always trusts, always hopes, always perseveres. Love never fails."
1 Corinthians 13:4–8a

Reflection Questions:

Have you ever encountered a Queen Bee? Think of a few examples. How did those instances make you feel?

What are your thoughts and attitudes about women?

What is your history with other women?

How does this history inform your relationships now?

Queen Bees

What three characteristics do you dislike most in other women?

What three characteristics about your interactions with or thoughts toward women need the most improvement?

Action Plan!

Take a quick survey of your female relationships. Then decide which category best describes you. Do you have healthy relationships? If so, perhaps it's time for you to mentor a younger woman like God commands in Titus 2. Ask the Lord if this is something He wants you to begin.

Do you have nonexistent relationships? Do you rely solely on the company of other people such as men and family members? If so, pray about whom you need to be closer to, and ask the Lord to begin bringing godly female friendships into your life (this might mean making you less resistant to them).

Are your relationships with other women bad? (We'll say "in need of improvement")? Do you have relationships that seem fine on the surface, but have tension, bitterness, jealousy, or resentment underneath? Do you have women in your life who seem to be full-blown enemies? Do you secretly dislike the women in your life? If so, then *Dethroning the Queen* is especially for you! God wants to improve your relationships. If you are willing, then read on!

CHAPTER TWO

Untapped Potential: The Importance of Female Friendships

"Though one may be overpowered, two can defend themselves. A cord of three strands is not quickly broken."
ECCLESIASTES 4:12

ANTHROPOLOGY 101

WHILE I WAS TAKING an anthropology course as a sophomore in college, the professor assigned a book about chimpanzees. I was required to take the course to fulfill one of my many dreaded General Education prerequisites. While reading the book, I was mostly frustrated with the fact that this course had nothing at all to do with my life or career aspirations. Yet, one particular part of the book struck me deeply. It was the story of two female chimps that were best friends. Apparently, their bond was so deep that when something happened to one of them, the hurt one would run to the other. They would embrace each other and send out loud, piercing screams together. But the second they were done embracing and screaming, all the other chimpanzees, even the big males, would scatter across the grounds and run for safety. All the chimps knew that the two of them were about to shake things up and set stuff straight, which might even mean an attack!

That story resonated with me, because it caused me to think of the potential for power in female-female sisterhoods in the kingdom of God. It displays the power of unity. As women, we should be so safe with each other that we "scream" when one of our sisters in Christ "screams," and vice versa. Even the Bible tells us that we are to, "Rejoice with those who rejoice; mourn with those who mourn" (Romans 12:15). Just like those two female chimps were a force to be reckoned with when they were united and standing in one accord, imagine what a threat we would be to the enemy if we had that kind of bond! Imagine knowing that as soon as the enemy saw you consoling a hurt sister, he would run for safety from the power of your unity and the threat of your retaliation on someone else's behalf.

LIES FROM THE ENEMY

Unfortunately, the Devil knows our potential for strength, and he tries to break that strength by pitting us against one another. He knows we will never reach our full potential in Christ, or have nearly as much strength and power, if we are not bonded to the other women in the Kingdom. Have you ever heard women say things like, "I just don't like women," "I can't trust women because they've stabbed me in the back," or, "I've always been the type of person to have male friends instead of female friends"? Realize those ways of thinking are rooted in lies from the enemy. One of his tricks is to separate women with such beliefs. Having a preference for male company may seem understandable, and distrusting women may even seem justifiable; however, these habits play a subtle part in the Devil's grand scheme to separate the women of God.

Other times, it is not even the Devil that breaks up bonds between women. Much of the time we willingly battle one another. Far too often, instead of being a place of safety for other women, we are a place of antagonism. What should be a wall of fortitude made up of a body of godly women unified under Christ often becomes fractured by jealousy, competition, pride, and hatred, and that wall of fortitude crumbles into bits of gravel.

The story about the two female chimpanzees illustrates the importance of solidarity between women, which is particularly important in the kingdom of God. This solidarity principle has implications both for the corporate body as a whole (the church) and for our personal relationships with women.

THE BODY OF CHRIST: CORPORATE IMPLICATIONS

1 Corinthians 12:12 and 27 says, "The body is a unit, though it is made up of many parts; and though all its parts are many, they form one body. So it is with Christ... Now you are the body of Christ, and each one of you is a part of it." These verses tell us that we, believers, collectively make up the body of Christ. It also suggests that the body has functions. In the rest of chapter twelve, Paul goes on to describe the various functions of a body. A body has a foot, a hand, an ear, and an eye, and all these parts are important. The children of God all form one body, and we are supposed to function and act as one unit. Our walks with God are not independent from each other. We are all connected. We collectively are the body of Christ. It is not just that Suzy is the body of Christ, Jack is the body of Christ, and Rachel is the body of Christ, but the sum of us taken together is the body of Christ.

WE ARE INTER-DEPENDENT

First Corinthians 12:14 says, "Now the body is not made up of one part but of many," and verse twenty one says, "The eye cannot say to the hand, 'I don't need you!' And the head cannot say to the feet, 'I don't need you'." In other words, we need each other in order to function. An eye cannot function by itself; it only functions within the context of the body. Believers must work together. There is no getting around it. If we are not unified, we cannot function as a unit and will never be the church we are called to be. There are many various groups and divisions within the body, but one of those groups is women. Women of God must learn to be unified. Living in the Queen Bee mentality will only create division, and that division will limit the functioning of God's church!

Sometimes we are deceived and believe we are functioning well spiritually, when in reality we are not connected to other members of the body. In reality, we aren't functioning unless we're connected. It's like a bouquet of flowers cut from the branch. They appear to flourish for a little while, but since they are disconnected from their life source, it is only a matter of time before they die. The same goes for us. Ultimately, our life source is Christ, but we are still members of one body. The members of the body cannot function like cut stems in a glass vase forever. If we want to live up to our calling as a church, representing God accurately and doing His work fully, we need to be connected.

CANCER: AN UNSETTLING PARALLEL

Consider it this way. When we are not unified, we interfere with God's specially designed structure for the body of believers, automatically causing impaired functioning. Try to picture it as a physical body. I would hate to think the church would have cancer, gangrene, infections, and chronic illness! But when there is division, between women or between any other groups, that's essentially what happens to the body of Christ. It's uncanny how much the physical body can provide insight into spiritual matters. For instance, cancer is the abnormal and uncontrollable division of cells. All that uncontainable division is what causes the tumors that can often be fatal. If division is fatal in our physical bodies, how much more damaging is it in the body of believers? If cancer is what happens when the physical body experiences too much malignant division, imagine what happens to the body of believers when there is too much division among us. How can we be the light of the world if we need to be laid up in a hospital bed?

Now in no way am I suggesting that women are solely responsible for the division in the church. Nor am I undermining God's grace, which

Untapped Potential: The Importance of Female Friendships

thankfully delivers us out of our own hands and into God's. Rather, I believe that as God-fearing members of the Kingdom, we should consider the part we play in church division. Are not our Queen Bee interactions a major point of weakness?

Also consider this. In John 17, Jesus is praying for all believers. This is the last prayer He prays before He is arrested. Of all the things He could have prayed for before He was taken to be crucified, He made time to specifically pray for the unity of believers. He could have used that time to pray for our protection, provision, or healing, but He chose unity. That says a lot. Imagine Jesus in the Garden of Gethsemane. He's sweating drops of blood in anguish and using all the energy He can muster to pray, and then He says, "May they be brought to complete unity to let the world know that you sent me and have loved them even as you have loved me" (John 17:23). So think how grieved the Lord must be to see how we so often minimize the importance of unity. Jesus' prayer should inspire us to remain connected so we can communicate the message of God to the world.

INDIVIDUAL RELATIONSHIPS: PERSONAL IMPLICATIONS

We also need to be unified for personal reasons, aside from our functioning as the body of Christ. Why? Let's look at Ecclesiastes 4:9–12:

"Two are better than one, because they have a good return for their work: If one falls down, his friend can help him up. But pity the man who falls and has no one to help him up! Also, if two lie down together, they will keep warm. But how can one keep warm alone? Though one may be overpowered, two can defend themselves. A cord of three strands is not quickly broken."

Here we see several reasons why it is important for us to be unified with each other for the sake of our personal lives. Let's briefly identify them.

Dethroning the Queen

Productivity

Verse nine says, "Two are better than one, because they have a good return for their work." One person can only produce so much work a day, but with more than one, productivity is increased. Sometimes when I am in my kitchen cleaning alone, I take a long time. But when I had roommates and they were all in the kitchen cleaning with me, talking and playing music, we got the job done much more quickly. And not only that, but it was much more enjoyable!

Support & Encouragement

Ecclesiastes also talks about support in verse ten: "If one falls down, his friend can help him up." I lived in a house with four women after I graduated from college and we all went through bad days. Sometimes one of us would come home crying, or someone would be discouraged, depressed, or would even be encountering spiritual warfare. On those days, we as roommates and friends would be there for the hurting person, praying for her, encouraging her, and comforting her with the Word. It was invaluable. But, "Pity the man who falls and has no one to help him up!" (Ecclesiastes 4:10b).

Sustenance

"Also, if two lie down together, they will keep warm. But how can one keep warm alone?" (Ecclesiastes 4:11). We are also called to sustain each other. God sustains us, be we need to understand that one of the ways He sustains us is by working through others. When we are not unified with the other women in the kingdom of God, we are cutting off sources of sustenance. You cannot be down on the ground dying of cold and pray to the Lord to warm you when you're not connecting to your sisters in Christ. It is quite possible that God wants to warm you through your sisters.

Untapped Potential: The Importance of Female Friendships

Protection & Covering

Verse twelve gives us the next point, saying, "Two can defend themselves. A cord of three strands is not quickly broken." Let me tell you, there have been times when the only thing that got me through was the spiritual covering and protection my sisters in Christ provided me. They are my best friends. I have faced some of the biggest tragedies of my life with them right there with me. Once when I was sitting on my bed in a heap crying in deep pain, my three roommates came and sat on my bed and surrounded me. Two of them came to either side of me, and the third one came from behind me and lifted me up with her hands. The three of them prayed for me when all I could do was cry. I remember how powerful that day was. I was covered. I was shielded from the enemy's attacks at a time when I was spiritually vulnerable. As a result, I got through a very dark time.

It is so crucial for every one of us to have those kinds of relationships. The sad thing is, a lot of us go through things, but because we are not unified with our sisters, we take hits we're not supposed to take and get knocked down when we're not supposed to get knocked down, all because we forfeit a certain amount of strength and covering when we forfeit relationships with women. But when you are of one accord with your sisters, the presence of God is there (Matthew 18:20). In the midst of unity, there is strength and a formidable presence against which the enemy cannot stand.

Purpose

Another reason we need to be unified with our sisters in Christ is to help fulfill our purpose. Ephesians 2:10 says, "For we are God's workmanship, created in Christ Jesus to do good works, which God prepared in advance for us to do." "Works" refers to purpose, and each one of us has it. The thing is, not being unified with your sisters will inhibit your purpose. How? Well, as we have established in chapter one, the Queen Bee dynamic between women is sinful; and sin inhibits purpose. That is why the writer in Hebrews 12 says, "Let us throw off everything that hinders and the sin that so easily entangles, and let us run with perseverance the race marked out for us" (Hebrews 12:1). In order for the people of God to live out their faith fully, we must rid ourselves of weighty sin. Imagine running a marathon with a 100-pound weight. Think of trying to run with ropes or netting entangled around your legs. Well, that's what we do when we try to walk out our faith while maintaining sinful Queen Bee issues. After all, Galatians 5:20, 21 makes it clear that "hatred, discord, jealousy, fits of rage, selfish ambition, dissensions, factions and envy," which are often so prevalent in our female relationships, are all part of the sinful nature. Often we think murder, stealing, and sexual sin are the big problems. But Galatians warns us that these Queen Bee issues are just as serious, and "those who live like this will not inherit the Kingdom of God" (Galatians 5:21).

While unhealthy relationships inhibit purpose, healthy relationships assist purpose. In Luke 10, Jesus sends out seventy-two disciples He had appointed. In verse one, it says He "sent them two by two." I believe that detail is significant. Jesus did not send His disciples out into the world to fulfill His work alone—He sent them in pairs. There are many examples of this sort of thing in Scripture. When the Holy Spirit releases Paul for ministry in Acts 13, He sends Barnabas with him. And later, when Paul is writing to Timothy, he sends for Mark, saying, "He is helpful to me in my ministry" (2 Timothy 4:11). When Mary was pregnant with Jesus, she ran to her cousin Elizabeth, who was pregnant with John the Baptist. There are many other examples you will find in Scripture, but the point is that positive, healthy, godly relationships with other women will help you live out your God-given purpose. That can only happen once you get rid of Queen Bee characteristics.

In Conclusion: Tapping into Potential

As women, we should learn from those two chimpanzees. Like them, we should strive for such unity that when one of us cries, all of us cry. That solidarity would defy what people say about women not getting along,

Untapped Potential: The Importance of Female Friendships

and I believe it would confuse and frighten the enemy so much that he would have no choice but to run and hide in fear of what an army of united women of God can do! God has a mighty work prepared for His daughters. There are those who should teach, encourage, evangelize, write, heal, minister, serve, and do all sorts of labor for the Kingdom. Together, we can be the body and the women of God that God has appointed to labor for the Kingdom, and when we dethrone the Queen Bee nature in our hearts and come together in one accord, we are free to experience the abundance of strength, support, joy, and encouragement that comes from godly sisterhood!

Prayer

Dear Heavenly Father,
Thank You for the truth of Your Word. Thank You for promising to give me comfort, support, protection, companionship, and so much more. Lord, You care about relationships, and I know there are so many wonderful things You want me to experience through relationships. Lord, I want to experience Your love fully and be a healthy part of Your Kingdom. So please start mending my heart and my relationships with women right now in the Name of Jesus. God, You've promised that Your Holy Spirit would guide me, so I pray You would do that as I let You dethrone Queen Bee characteristics in me and in my relationships. And I thank and praise You in advance with faith that You are already beginning to do it. Thank You for how much of my potential I will experience as my relationships with women get better. I pray these things in Jesus' Precious Name. Amen.

Memory Verse

"The body is a unit, though it is made up of many parts; and though all its parts are many, they form one body."
1 CORINTHIANS. 12:12a

Dethroning the Queen

Reflection Questions

Meditate on the words in 1 Corinthians 12:12–27 and let its truth sink into your spirit. What does Paul mean when he says we are one body?

What does this passage tell you about having a successful spiritual life?

What are some of the unproductive areas of your life? Where could you benefit from stronger female relationships?

Action Plan!

List the women you need to connect, reconnect, or reconcile with. Pray for them this week, and ask the Lord to begin opening healthy streams of communication between you. If you find this challenging, describe this difficulty to the Lord in detail, or write about it, and then ask the Holy Spirit to help you.

CHAPTER THREE

The Queen of Comparison

"Each one should test his own actions. Then he can take pride in herself,
without comparing himself to somebody else."
GALATIANS 6:4

I WAS IN MY ROOM getting dressed to go out to church one evening. I was especially excited because there was going to be a youth service for the teenagers from my church and the surrounding neighborhood, and I was looking forward to having a great time and seeing all my friends. (You know how important socializing is for teenagers, even in church). I put on a cute, fitted white shirt that matched the brand new, recently purchased grey and white skirt that I loved. I finished the outfit off with a pair of white, strappy sandals and my favorite silver hoop earrings. I thought the outfit was very flattering on me. My hair had reached a nice length, longer than usual, so I combed it out so it would hang long in the back and swept the top up with a band. (My mom always told me that bringing my hair off my face was a pretty look for me). I applied a little bit of lip-gloss and smiled into the mirror. It was one of those really good days, when everything worked. I was pleased—I looked great!

When I arrived at church, I was excited and in a great mood. (You know that as women we just feel especially good on those days when we are happy with the way we look). My best friend was there and we immediately latched on to each other as best friends do and headed for the women's restroom. Girls tended to go to the restroom ceremonially before every social event. We stood together in the mirror laughing and talking eagerly about the evening. My best friend was primping, so I pulled out my lip-gloss and lip liner to follow suit (though I had just applied some not ten minutes before).

While we were standing in front of the mirror, Layla, the third member of our trio, walked in. She was a gorgeous girl with thick, dark hair, brown eyes, and bronzy skin. Everyone shrieked, "Hi!" and hugged, then the three of us went back to the mirror and Layla began performing her last-minute touch-ups while the three of us chatted away. The talk and giggles subsided while we finished checking our faces. I looked at Layla in the mirror. She pulled a small black compact from out of her purse, wiped her applicator around in the soft, tan foundation, and began smoothing powder around her cheeks. She was also wearing eye shadow, mascara, and lipstick, forms of makeup that I hadn't ventured into yet.

Suddenly, something happened. I didn't feel as cute anymore. My shiny, clear lip-gloss now seemed to pale in comparison to Layla's powder, shadow, and liner. My little bit of natural-colored lip liner looked simple and foolish. I looked plain, like a little girl. My grey and white skirt was lackluster against Layla's black shirt and dark jeans. My face seemed drab and lacking in color. My hair didn't even compensate. And my outfit, the one I had been thrilled about five seconds earlier, now seemed completely boring and unattractive. I searched in the mirror for the cute girl I had seen when I was alone in my room, but I could no longer see her. All my previous excitement had come crashing to the floor, and I felt unsatisfactory. In a matter of seconds, my entire perception of myself had turned around one hundred and eighty degrees.

COMPARISON. It is a major downfall for thousands of women. It's something I know many of us have practiced, experienced, and wrestled with for years. As women, we seem to have a knack for comparing ourselves to others, and we often do it so much that it becomes second nature to us. In fact, it does not always seem like a stronghold, because it comes so naturally. Comparison is a habit, and unfortunately it is one of the unhealthiest habits we have. A woman walks into a room and we examine her entire outfit and compare it to our own. We see models and actresses on television whose bodies become the gauges against which we measure our own bodies. A man we're attracted to starts dating someone, and we study her personality and mannerisms and contrast them with ours. We compare talent. We compare wealth. We compare hair types. We compare skin colors. We compare achievements. We compare careers. We compare families. We compare ministries. We compare spiritual gifts. We compare worship styles. We even go so far as to compare spirituality and our walks with the Lord. We can compare anything. It can be physical, material, mental, intangible, emotional, or spiritual. It can be something deep or something shallow, something negative, or something positive, something petty, or something serious. It doesn't matter what it is for us personally; comparison can be applied to anything.

Sometimes we compare subconsciously. It can be as small as a shift in our mood as soon as we hear good news about someone else. It can also be an obvious stronghold in our lives. Neither form of comparison is healthy. It does not matter how big or small, noticeable or unnoticeable our comparison is. What matters is whether comparison is in our hearts, for the Bible says the Word of God "judges the thoughts and attitudes of the heart" (Hebrews 4:12).

PROBLEMS WITH COMPARISON

Although comparison is something very common to many of us, we don't always understand exactly what comparison is and the various factors that come into play whenever we compare ourselves to someone else. Having a decent understanding of comparison will help us to see how unhealthy and ungodly this habit is, and will be critical if we are to identify and dethrone the Queen of Comparison in our own lives.

Dethroning the Queen

Comparison Makes Differences into Flaws

When we compare, we temporarily make something else the standard, so if we are different from that standard in any way, we believe ourselves to be flawed or inferior. Here's an example. One of my absolute favorite television shows is *America's Next Top Model*.[1] From watching that show, I saw how specific body types are ideal for certain types of modeling. Some models have angular, androgynous bodies. They have thin arms and legs, straight torsos, and flat chests. That sort of boyish body type seems to be ideal for high fashion editorial photo shoots where the models must come up with "edgy" poses. During those photo shoots, the curvier models have to hunch their backs and bend their knees to achieve that "edgy" look, while the models with the boyish, angular bodies tend to have an advantage. But when it came to lingerie photo shoots, the models with curvier bodies often have the advantage while the other models must try harder to arch their backs and push their hips out in order to create the illusion of curves. I realized the models' bodies do not look alike, yet those differences are good, because different bodies are ideal for different looks. The curvy model does not have to compare her body to that of the angular model, because the curvy model's body is great for modeling as well. Comparison would have taken the curvy model's eyes off of her own strengths. If she had felt inadequate because her body lacked the androgynous element of the model next to her, then her view of reality would have been distorted. The curvy model's body is not inadequate, it is simply different. But the lie of comparison is that difference is inadequacy. When we compare ourselves to others, we are tempted to believe we are flawed when we are different. For that very reason, comparison can be extremely unhealthy, because not all differences are problems, but comparison will always tell us otherwise.

Comparison is contrary to God's will. The Bible clearly teaches that God designs people differently, because each person is designed to serve a specific and necessary function. We will talk more about that concept later in the chapter, but first, let's look at some more underlying problems with comparison.

Comparison Takes our Eyes off our Strengths

Not only does comparison make us feel like our differences are inadequacies, but comparison also takes our eyes off of our strengths.

One of my closest friends and I were talking one day, and during the course of our conversation, we found out both of us had secretly been comparing our personalities to the other person's and had, at some point, wished we could be more like the other. I greatly admire how entertaining and gregarious my friend is. There is never a dull moment with her. She always has something to talk about, and is known for bursting into the room with an explosion of laughter and funny stories. In addition, she is a leader and a communicator, so she usually verbalizes her thoughts and is always striking up deep conversations based on some concept she's been recently thinking about. I think of her as having a big personality, which for someone like me can be a lot to handle, but I admire it a lot because I see how much people are drawn to her. She is the life of the party at social events and people tend to contact her when they want to know what is going on. It seemed to me that everyone liked her and wanted to be around her.

Many times, I would find myself comparing my personality to hers, thinking men would be more attracted to someone with her extremely energetic and entertaining qualities. At times, I would even fear that because my personality was not like hers, I would miss out on friendships and even romantic relationships!

When I told her about these things, she was astonished. She could not believe that for months I had felt that way. In addition, I found out she had compared her personality to mine! My friend and I are similar in many ways, but there are certain aspects of our personalities that are very different. I love to laugh and have fun (which is part of the reason why I actually like my friend's personality), but I am much more reserved than she is. I rarely verbalize my thoughts without first thinking them over in my head for a substantial period of time. I have a tendency to listen deeply and observe my surroundings, process the information in my mind, and then state my opinion some time later. In fact, many of my opinions are not verbalized, because I tend to keep them to myself unless I feel they are necessary to share (as opposed to some people who share their opinions unless they are necessary to withhold). I open up and play, laugh, and joke with my friends, but I am not nearly as outgoing with strangers as I am with the people I know and am comfortable around. When I compared these characteristics to my friend's, I was tempted to think of them as shortcomings that would hinder my relationships with others and make me less attractive to new people. But as it turns out, my friend had always admired those qualities about me. She said, "I always wished I could be the mysterious girl in the corner, but it's just not me. And sometimes I tried to be that way, but I couldn't. I always thought guys liked the girls who were quiet and mysterious, and I worried that I was so goofy that men wouldn't be attracted to me."

Isn't it funny how the very thing I thought was a weakness in myself was the thing she saw as a strength in me? And the very thing I saw as a strength in her was the thing she had seen as a weakness in herself? Well, that is exactly how comparison works. Comparison takes your eyes off of your strengths. That often happens when we fixate on the specific strengths of someone we admire. But often, we don't have the same assets as another person. We have our own assets. My friend had to learn to prize her exuberant personality, while I had to prize my reserved one. We had to learn to admire each other's strong points without becoming blind to our own.

Comparison Creates an Unstable Sense of Self

When I was a teenager standing in the mirror in the women's restroom at my church, my self-perception changed. Next to Layla, I felt unsatisfactory. Yet ten minutes earlier, I was very happy with the way I looked. Had I not seen myself before I got to church? Was the mirror in the women's restroom distorted? No, my perception was distorted. Layla's presence did not change anything about the way I actually looked. The only difference was the fact that I chose to compare myself. And that one difference made a huge impact on me.

When you compare yourself, you become a slave to your environment. The environment has the ability to bring you high, or bring you low, because your self-assessment is dependent on how you measure up to those around you. And since there are constantly different people around, your self-esteem constantly fluctuates. It can cause you to experience both false pride and false insecurity.

False Insecurity

False insecurity can happen in many ways. A woman is very attractive, so you start feeling unattractive. A woman is a great leader in the church, so you feel spiritually immature. A woman's husband brings her a huge bouquet of flowers every week, and you start thinking your husband doesn't love you. A woman has a great big house and a luxurious car, so you start thinking your things are shabby. A woman has a charismatic and outgoing personality, and you suddenly feel boring. A woman is very delicate, so you conclude that you are tomboyish. She gets compliments all the time, and you think there is something wrong with you. Negative comparison plays out in all kinds of situations, but the basic principle in all of them is: comparing yourself to people you admire will often create a false sense of insecurity.

False Pride

Another problem some of us deal with is comparison-based pride. This problem is tricky because it is not an obvious form of insecurity, but is a form of insecurity nonetheless. Some women walk around feeling great about themselves because of what they put their stock in. Pride can boast in anything, so it can be about relationships, clothes, businesses, jobs, beauty, body type, intelligence, leadership, spirituality, families, or anything else. And sometimes the reason women take pride in themselves is because they are surrounded by women who seem to be in some way inferior to them! If you have ever experienced this type of comparison-based self-esteem, consider this. Self-worth is not valid if it only exists relative to other people's weaknesses and shortcomings. For example, have you ever noticed how a five-year-old kindergartner can feel really smart around a toddler? Around the toddler, the kindergartner takes on a bossy or condescending tone of voice and starts correcting the toddler's recitation of her ABCs, or starts boasting about how she can count to a higher number than the toddler. But put this same bragging kindergartner around a fifth grader who has mastered fractions and long division and the kindergartner feels inferior. Pride can always be trumped! That's why it's not true self-worth; it's only an illusion of self-worth created by comparing oneself to other people's weaknesses (And notice how unsisterly such behavior is!).

Comparison is an Insufficient Measure

Relative judgments (judgments that do not exist without a standard of comparison) can never give us an accurate measure of our value. For instance, words like "better," "worse," "bigger," "smaller," "more," and "less" only exist within the context of comparison, but those words alone cannot give accurate, defining information about an object.

Imagine it this way. Say you get pulled over by a police officer who is ticketing speeding drivers. He writes you a speeding ticket, and on the line that indicates how fast you were going he writes, "Faster than the blue Honda." You would be infuriated! And why? Because his assessment is merely a comparison. Just because you were driving faster than the blue Honda does not mean you were speeding. That is why police officers have

The Queen of Comparison

a device in their cars that can detect how fast cars are actually going. It is not relative; it is objective and measures speed based on distance covered over time (mph). If you are driving at 50 mph, it does not matter if you are faster or slower than the blue Honda. What matters is the speed limit. If the speed limit is 30 mph, then you can agree that you were speeding and deserve to get a ticket. But if the speed limit were 55 mph, then you would know you were ticketed unjustly.

The car analogy is almost ridiculously obvious, but why can't we understand this concept with people? We cannot determine how we measure up in our looks, jobs, cars, spirituality, or success by comparing ourselves to the people around us. What matters is how we measure up in God's sight. Yet, too often, particularly as women, we somehow start letting our sense of self be measured by how we compare to women around us. Comparison is just as insufficient to accurately measure people as it is to accurately measure auto speed.

The Fundamental Problem: Comparison Deceives

You should notice that comparison is deceptive. It skews our perceptions and causes us to believe things about ourselves (positive or negative) that are not true, or perform faulty measures of ourselves. Always beware of deception. It is one of humanity's biggest pitfalls, and always opens up a myriad of other problems because it leads us away from the truth without our awareness.

IMPACT ON FEMALE RELATIONSHIPS

It is easy to see how comparison has a negative impact on our personal lives, but it is also extremely detrimental in female relationships. Comparison has the ability to tear us apart. Comparison is an internal issue, residing in our hearts and in our minds. But even though it is often unseen, it remains a major threat to the kingdom of God because of its potential to divide.

Dethroning the Queen

Causes Vulnerability and Superficiality

1 Corinthians 13:7 says, "[Love] always trusts." But it is very challenging to have healthy, open, trusting relationships with other women when we are constantly comparing ourselves to them. For example, sometimes the low self-esteem that results from comparison causes us to feel too vulnerable to open up and be real with other women. We feel inferior, and we fear exposing that weak area because we don't want to be hurt, disrespected, or humiliated. As a defense, we create superficial relationships or friendships where only certain aspects of ourselves are shown. But the level of unity and fellowship that God desires His women to have is much deeper than the superficial relationships we often create. The truth is that we are supposed to be vulnerable with each other without fear of judgment or attack. That's why the Bible says, "Love always trusts." Satan likes to keep women from experiencing that fellowship, because he knows the strength and edification others bring into our lives is a threat to him. He uses comparison because it is a major threat to meaningful relationships. It creates insecurity and discomfort that hinders our ability to be real with others. That's why it is critical that we not let issues such as comparison interfere with our relationships with women in the Kingdom.

Causing Resentment

When we go day after day feeling inferior, overlooked, undervalued, and incomplete in comparison to another person, after a while, our flesh naturally develops resentment toward that person. Siblings often display that kind of resentment. I remember one time when my brother, Aaron, and I were playing video games. I was about seven years old, and Aaron was five. Being the older sibling, I was the winner most of the time. (Older siblings tend to have an unfair advantage because of their age and further developed skills.) Well, I would beat him game after game. One particular day, I suppose he decided he'd had enough of being the underdog. The game had just ended and with a mocking smile, I triumphantly declared, "I win!" In his frustration, Aaron grabbed his controller and chucked it at me! (Now I was not entirely the victim in this story—no doubt I had deserved the hit due to my constant instigating and boasting, but we will talk about pride in chapter twelve). The point is that comparison can lead to resentment. We get tired of coming up short in comparison to others, and if we are not careful, we will direct that frustration toward other women and start resenting them. That resentment can take place both in our actions and in our hearts.

Causing Envy

1 Corinthians 13:4 says, "[Love] does not envy." I believe one of the biggest problems women deal with is envy. The Bible is clear that desiring and feeling threatened by what other people have always creates major problems. We will discuss jealousy in-depth in chapter five, but one of the ways envy gets into our hearts is through comparison. Comparison is one of the main precursors to envy, because it causes us to focus on what other people have and what we lack. We look at other women's qualities, characteristics, talents, accomplishments, relationships, lifestyles, and possessions, and then we compare them to our own. If we come up short in comparison, it is only natural to become envious. Nobody likes feeling inferior, but instead of healthily dealing with our tendency to compare, we often move on to envy.

Many times envy will go after the thing that makes us feel inferior. For example, if another woman's looks make us feel inferior, then our hearts desire those looks. If another woman's talent makes us feel inferior, then we envy and desire her talent. No matter what we feel we lack, comparison makes us feel as though we are deficient or incomplete, so we envy something another woman has in our attempt to make up the lack. That comparison-driven envy creates deep and deadly divides between women.

Dethroning the Queen

Gossip and Slander

Sometimes we go another route, and instead of desiring what another woman has, we find ways to tear her down so we don't feel so bad about ourselves. (As you can see, these issues link up quite a bit! We discuss slander in chapter ten.) Since we can't take away her money, success, good looks, or popularity, we cut her down with our mouths instead. We compensate for her achievements by finding ways to magnify her flaws. We speak negatively about her. Instead of agreeing when someone points out her good qualities, we add, "Yeah, but…" to every compliment. It is a way of tricking ourselves into believing that she is the one with flaws, not us. After all, comparison insults our pride! So instead of wrestling with our insecurity, we project it onto the other person by emphasizing her weaknesses. Slandering someone else makes us feel more powerful, so insecure people use it as a weapon. Often, women with low self-esteem try to empower themselves in an unhealthy, ungodly way by verbally tearing others down.

As a schoolgirl, I was a little bit of a bookworm. I enjoyed reading, I always did my homework, and I loved raising my hand in class when I knew the answer to the teacher's questions. Coincidentally, I was known as the "Teacher's Pet." There was one particular girl who always made fun of me. I would hand in my homework or solve a math problem on the board, and she'd be at her desk mimicking me. At recess, she would find ways to tease me mercilessly. I would come home with pounding headaches some days, or go cry in the girl's restroom from something she said. My mother finally asked me, "What kind of grades does this girl get?" I told her she had a hard time in class, and seemed to always get C's on tests (somehow people's grades got around after math quizzes and such). My mother exclaimed, "Well, of course she makes fun of you!" I didn't understand. My mother explained, "When people are immature and have low self-esteem, they want to make other people feel bad. She teases you about your grades because you get straight A's, and that makes her feel bad about herself. She teases you about being 'skinny', but she is obviously uncomfortable being so much heavier than you. Since she's immature, she tries to make you feel like you're the one with all the problems, when really she's the one who feels inferior."

Slander and gossip are hurtful. Comparison especially can drive woman to speak hurtful words against women they feel threatened by, and that process causes major division between women.

We all know this dynamic does not stop at the playground or even in the secular world. Even women in church struggle with this principle. Unfortunately, a lot of women grow up, but don't grow out of this kind of immaturity. Rather, they go on comparing themselves to other women and responding with gossip and slander to combat their own low self-esteem. Sometimes, I think we women can be just as bad as little girls, we just learn how to disguise our attacks better. We pass off masked criticisms. We praise in public and rebuke behind backs. We do it because if we were to be completely honest, we are the ones who feel deficient. We are the ones who feel insecure. We are the ones who feel inferior when we compare ourselves to other women, and instead of getting rid of comparison, we try to level the playing field by bringing the other woman down.

Thriving When Others Are Weak

This might be the most profound way comparison tears women apart, even more than by making us fear vulnerability, or causing us to be resentful, envious, or malicious in our speech. 1 Corinthians 13:6 says, "Love does not delight in evil but rejoices with the truth." Comparison creates an environment where we thrive when other people are weak. The little girl in school feels better when the teacher's pet starts getting C's on her assignments. The coworker feels better when the employee of the month gets laid off. The minister feels better when the other woman's ministry suffers. The depressed wife feels better when the other married couple goes through a separation. The women at the party are more comfortable when that woman spills punch all over her beautiful white dress. The lonely woman is happy when the popular woman is abandoned. It's always a huge red flag when we rejoice in the same things that the Devil rejoices in. Rejoicing in the misfortune of others is in extreme opposition with Kingdom-minded thinking, yet is often a byproduct of comparison.

Healthy armies or sports teams understand they are only as strong as their weakest link, but we deceive ourselves by thinking that other people's failures, problems, and mess-ups are advantageous to us. That perception makes it obvious that we are not thinking of ourselves as one body; rather, it shows we are a body that is weak, fragmented, divided, and sick. In 1 Corinthians 12:26, Paul says, "If one part suffers, every part suffers with it; if one part is honored, every part rejoices with it." Comparison is contrary to this principle. Too often, instead of thriving when others are thriving, we thrive when others are suffering, not out of cruelty, but because when others are suffering, we don't feel inferior to them in comparison.

COMBATING COMPARISON

Now that we understand a little bit more about what comparison is and the way it deceives us, let's look at some truths that we can hold onto and start combating comparison in our lives.

Variety is Good!

As we discussed earlier in the chapter, when we compare ourselves, we often feel insecure about our differences. We are tempted to believe our differences are flaws. In actuality, difference is vital. God created people with different talents, abilities, anointing, purpose, gifts, personalities, material things, and even looks, because there is purpose in variety. That concept is very true in the church. In 1 Corinthians 12, Paul talks to the Corinthians. Some of them had started feeling undervalued because they were not like other people in the church. I imagine there were ushers who felt insecure because their gifts were not like those of the prophets. Or there were administrators who felt inferior because they were not deacons. Praise and worship leaders felt lesser than teachers, and elders felt lesser than bishops. Paul came to set them straight by emphasizing that everyone is important, because each person is part of a larger unit that only functions successfully when everyone is operating in their unique and different gifts. Paul writes,

> Now the body is not made up of one part but of many. If the foot should say, "Because I am not a hand, I do not belong to the body," it would not for that reason cease to be part of the body. And if the ear should say, "Because I am not an eye, I do not belong to the body," it would not for that reason cease to be part of the body. If the whole body were an eye, where would the sense of hearing be? If the whole body were an ear, where would the sense of smell be? But in fact God has arranged the parts in the body, every one of them, just as he wanted them to be. If they were all one part, where would the body be? As it is, there are many parts, but one body (1 Corinthians 12:14–20).

Paul stresses that differences do not make people inferior, they make people necessary. Ushers are not less valuable than bishops merely because bishops have positions of authority. Everyone in the kingdom of God is important and needed. If everyone were bishops, who would organize, plan, facilitate, and keep things running smoothly? Everyone is needed. If only we could understand this principle!

This same principle operates on smaller scales as well. Not everyone can be partner at a law firm. Not everyone can be a fantastic singer. Not everyone can have the gift of teaching. Not everyone can be the leader. This concept is true in every way. Just think of how many different types of flowers there are—beauty comes in many shades! Not every woman should have long, flowing hair. Not every woman should have bronzy skin. Not every woman should be short, not every woman should be tall. Not every woman should be thin, not every woman should be curvy. Your uniqueness is an opportunity to add a deeper dimension to the world's beauty. Unfortunately, too many of us resent our differences, believing them to be flaws. We compare ourselves to others, and when we are different, we think there's something wrong with us. We need to understand that God delights in our differences, and that He ordained many of our differences to serve a vital function in this world.

Your Deficiencies Have a Function

Sometimes we compare ourselves to others and we do indeed find true deficiencies in ourselves. But sometimes these deficiencies balance out someone else's strong suits. I have a friend whom I feel at times is much more creative than I am. She thinks up activities on a whim and can stir up everyone else into a frenzy of excitement. At times, I am tempted to compare myself to her, because I am usually much more run-of-the-mill and conventional when it comes to thinking up ideas and activities. I tend to be conventional and traditional, so in comparison I often feel I am boring and uncreative. The truth is, my friend does have some creativity and eccentricity I don't, but when the two of us work together, my conventional nature works as a strength, not a weakness. I keep her creativity from going off the deep end. I help balance out some of her craziness and make sure the activities we plan are realistic and organized. Without my conservative influence, some of her activities would get out of hand and out of control. Or, they wouldn't even come to fruition at all, because where excitement inspires people to start a task, organization, planning, and caution are critical for successfully completing a task. So it is true I am not as creative as she is in certain ways, but what I sometimes perceive as my dullness can actually be a strength that brings the needed balance of organization and normalcy.

That's how God makes His people, particularly His women. We are an assortment of strengths and weaknesses that need to be balanced by each other. Like an actual body that needs all of its parts, we are designed to be interdependent. We do have weaknesses, but those weaknesses are not meant to be sources of comparison. Instead of comparing ourselves and being pulled farther apart from one another, we should seek to build partnerships where other people balance out our weaknesses and benefit from our strengths.

Test Yourself

Bad habits don't only add negative practices to our lives, but they also get in the way of good practices. Comparison works that way. Comparison is an ungodly means of self-evaluation, and so it gets in the way of healthy evaluation. Self-evaluation is an extremely needed activity in the lives of believers, for the Bible says, "But if we judged ourselves, we would not come under judgment. When we are judged by the Lord, we are being disciplined so that we will not be condemned with the world" (1 Corinthians 11:31, 32). When we judge ourselves, we are in the position to repent, eradicate sin, and strive for righteousness. Without self-evaluation, there would be no way to confess our shortcomings to God.

Comparison is the wrong way to assess yourself, but Galatians 6:4 reveals the right way when it says, "Each one should test his own actions. Then he can take pride in himself, without comparing himself to somebody else." According to the Bible, the way for us to evaluate ourselves is not to compare, but to test our actions. If you want to know how strong you are, you don't arm wrestle a weakling, you test your strength by seeing how large a weight you can lift. If you want to know how fast you can run, you don't race against other people and judge based on who came in first or second, you run a mile and time how long it took for you to complete the run. Believers have a way to test their actions, too. The answer is in 2 Timothy 3:16, 17, which says, "All Scripture is God-breathed and is useful for teaching, rebuking, correcting and training in righteousness, so that the man of God may be thoroughly equipped for every good work." The Word of God is our tester!

I believe some of us resort to comparison because we don't have enough Word in us to know whether or not we measure up, so we do all we know how to do and compare ourselves to other people. I want to tell you that comparison to other men or women will never give you an accurate report. An accurate report will only come from God's Word, and Jesus is the only person perfect enough to measure ourselves against, and it is His Word that we use as a tool for self-evaluation. It does not matter how anointed, how called, how mature, how old, how wise, how gifted, how strong, or how knowledgeable a person is. Scripture tells us we are to judge ourselves against the Word of God. The Word, not other people. The Word is a conduit through which God can speak to us about ourselves. And notice, whereas comparison is a flakey, wishy-washy, and unstable foundation for self-perception, the Word of God is precise, accurate, and cutting. According to Hebrews 4:12, it penetrates, divides, and judges. When we test ourselves against the Word of God, we have no need to compare ourselves.

Romans 12:3 says, "Think of yourself with sober judgment, in accordance with the measure of faith God has given you." Sober judgment suggests clarity of mind. Comparison clouds the mind. In order to truly test ourselves, we must abandon comparison and get into the truth of the Living Word. His truth will give us a sober-minded view of others and ourselves.

Your Worth Is in Christ

Comparison can shake us up when we don't have a solid foundation. Therefore the last element, which is absolutely essential in dethroning the Queen, is for us to know who we are in Christ. When we do, we don't need to rely on faulty measures like comparison to evaluate ourselves.

Learning who we are in Christ and walking in that security takes time and practice that cannot simply be written about in a book. It is vital that

The Queen of Comparison

you cultivate your relationship with God by spending time in His presence and reading His word, so truth can take root in your heart. The words of this chapter cannot replace that process, so I strongly encourage you, whether you are a seasoned Christian or new to the faith, to be consistent and constant in your time with the Lord. That way there is no room for the lies of the enemy to take root. Whenever we stray away from the presence of the Lord, we see ourselves with the eyes of our flesh, instead of the eyes of the Spirit. Only with eyes of the Spirit can we truly see who we are in Christ. Jeremiah the prophet warned us, saying, "Cursed is the one who trusts in man, who depends on flesh for his strength... But blessed is the man who trusts in the Lord, whose confidence is in him" (Jeremiah 17:5, 7). Comparing is like trusting in flesh, because it forces you to rely on people to tell you who you are and what your worth is. Instead, we need to trust in the Lord, and like it says in the Scripture, we must put our confidence in Him. We are only able to do that when we walk with Him, and learn who we are in His sight.

Here are some truths from the Word of God that you can begin to meditate on as you learn to dethrone the Queen of Comparison:

1. You are royalty.
2. You are fearfully and wonderfully made.
3. You are unconditionally loved.

Each of these truths exists because of your relationship to God. When you truly receive and believe them, you are in a much better position to release unhealthy habits like comparison. We will really spend time deepening our understanding of these points as we prepare to conclude this book in chapter thirteen. For now, really make it a point to be in the Lord's presence so He can speak to you about who you really are, and so you can get a true sense of your worth.

Are you tired of wrestling with low self-esteem and insecurity that comes from comparing yourself to others? Are you tired of constantly battling in your mind? Do you want to invite the truth of God's Word into your life and into your heart, to cut down the lies planted by seeds of comparison? If you are ready to dethrone the reign of comparison in your life, then pray this prayer with us.

Prayer

Dear Heavenly Father,
Thank You for Your Word that establishes my worth and value. Your Word frees me from the lies of comparison. So Lord, I repent for letting comparison reign in my heart. You are the only One who has authority over my life, so I dethrone comparison and I give You back Your rightful place. Forgive me for giving way to low self-esteem. Forgive me for resenting those I've compared myself to, and for letting comparison place distance between my sisters and myself in Christ. Forgive me for sinning against my sisters, and against You by comparing myself. And Lord, I know You forgive me, so I pray also that You would help me to forgive other women who compare themselves to me. I also ask that You give me the grace to change as I strive to die to comparison. Give me the strength to test my own actions, and to practice sober judgment, so that I have an accurate and healthy sense of self that does not waver in the presence of other people. And give me a greater understanding of my unique strengths, virtues, and great worth in your sight. I have all faith that You will do this so my life might bring greater glory to You, and I give you all the thanks and praise. In the power of Jesus' Precious Name, I pray. Amen.

Memory Verse

"Each one should test his own actions. Then he can take pride in himself, without comparing himself to somebody else."
GALATIANS 6:4

The Queen of Comparison

Reflection Questions

To whom do you compare yourself?

Do you ever feel bad about yourself due to comparing yourself to someone else? If yes, in what ways?

Do you ever inflate your worth and your strengths because of someone else's weaknesses? If yes, in what ways?

What are some of your true strengths? How do these differ from the "strengths" listed in question #3?

What are some of your actual weaknesses? How do these differ from the "weaknesses" listed in question #2?

Are you ready to dethrone the Queen of Comparison and start basing your worth in God's Word and testing your actions against God's Word?

Dethroning the Queen

Action Plan!

Write down the names of people you need to stop comparing yourself to. Then write down the three biggest areas that tempt you to compare yourself to others. Next to each one, write one true, positive fact that will never change and is therefore not subject to comparison. (For example, you might write something like, "Area 1: Looks—I have beautiful brown eyes! Area 2: Talents—God has called me to be a singer, not a dancer!" etc.)

CHAPTER FOUR

The Queen of Competition

"I have had a great struggle with my sister."
GENESIS 30:8

"JACOB LAY WITH RACHEL also, and he loved Rachel more than Leah. And he worked for Laban another seven years. When the Lord saw that Leah was not loved, he opened her womb, but Rachel was barren. Leah became pregnant and gave birth to a son. She named him Reuben, for she said, "It is because the Lord has seen my misery. Surely my husband will love me now." She conceived again, and when she gave birth to a son she said, "Because the Lord heard that I am not loved, he gave me this one too." So she named him Simeon. Again she conceived, and when she gave birth to a son she said, "Now at last my husband will become attached to me, because I have borne him three sons." So he was named Levi. She conceived again, and when she gave birth to a son she said, "This time I will praise the Lord." So she named him Judah. Then she stopped having children.

When Rachel saw that she was not bearing Jacob any children, she became jealous of her sister. So she said to Jacob, "Give me children, or I'll die!" Jacob became angry with her and said, "Am I in the place of God, who has kept you from having children?" Then she said, "Here is Bilhah, my maidservant. Sleep with her so that she can bear children for me and that through her I too can build a family." So she gave him her servant Bilhah as a wife. Jacob slept with her, and she became pregnant and bore him a son. Then Rachel said, "God has vindicated me; he has listened to my plea and given me a son." Because of this she named him Dan. Rachel's servant Bilhah conceived again and bore Jacob a second son. Then Rachel said, "I have had a great struggle with my sister, and I have won." So she named him Naphtali. When Leah saw that she had stopped having children, she took her maidservant Zilpah and gave her to Jacob as a wife. Leah's servant Zilpah bore Jacob a son. Then Leah said, "What good fortune!" So she named him Gad. Leah's servant Zilpah bore Jacob a second son. Then Leah said, "How happy I am! The women will call me happy." So she named him Asher.

During wheat harvest, Reuben went out into the fields and found some mandrake plants, which he brought to his mother Leah. Rachel said to Leah, "Please give me some of your son's mandrakes." But she said to her, "Wasn't it enough that you took away my husband? Will you take my son's mandrakes too?" "Very well," Rachel said, "he can sleep with you tonight in return for your son's mandrakes." So when Jacob came in from the fields that evening, Leah went out to meet him. "You must sleep with me," she said. "I have hired you with my son's mandrakes." So he slept with her that night.

God listened to Leah, and she became pregnant and bore Jacob a fifth son. Then Leah said, "God has rewarded me for giving my maidservant to my husband." So she named him Issachar. Leah conceived again and bore Jacob a sixth son. Then Leah said, "God has presented me with a precious gift. This time my husband will treat me with honor, because I have borne him six

The Queen of Competition

sons." So she named him Zebulun. Some time later she gave birth
to a daughter named Dinah.

Then God remembered Rachel; he listened to her and opened
her womb. She became pregnant and gave birth to a son and said,
"God has taken away my disgrace." She named him Joseph, and
said, "May the Lord add to me another son."

GENESIS 29:30–30:24

Above is a story of two sisters whose relationship suffered because of
their struggle with one major problem: competition. Sadly, many modern
day female relationships look like Rachel and Leah's—of rivalry, opposition, and strife. Competition is a major Queen Bee characteristic that tears
many female relationships apart. If more women understood the full
nature of competition and how it's both detrimental and fruitless, perhaps
less of us would engage in it.

DEFINING COMPETITION

The New International Webster's Concise Dictionary defines the word
compete this way: "To contend with another or others for a prize, superiority, etc."[1] Based on this definition, we see two dimensions of competition. The first is contest, and the second is status or reward.

THE CONTEST. In order for competition to exist, there must be some
sort of contest. Competition only exists within the context of opposition.
It's one person against the other. I like to picture competition as a board
game where players are racing against each other to the end. The contest
element of competition is the part of the game that is Red Piece vs. Blue
Piece. Top Hat vs. Thimble. Miss Scarlet vs. Mrs. Peacock. There are
always, to some degree, enemies or adversaries in competition.
Competition in games can be intense or lighthearted, but either way, there
is some sort of contest that sets one person against the other.

THE STATUS. There is also a status element in competition. In a game, you are trying to win. You are trying to finish first, or with the most points, the highest score, the fastest speed, or the most money. The goal is to finish with some sort of reward—even if it's nothing but being able to jump up and triumphantly declare, "I win!" Someone who is competing desires to come out with a prize, but the prize must distinguish the person above her opponents. Therefore, the end result of competition, in theory, is defeat of an opponent. Not only are the two players set against each other, but in the end, one will be exalted above the other, usually granting the victor a prize as well as a title. So, both contest and status play a part in competition.

What Do Women Compete Over?

The short answer is—everything. A woman can compete about absolutely anything. It can be who has the best job, who has the finest spouse or boyfriend, who has the longer hair, who has the biggest bra size, who cooks the best, who cleans the best, who knows the latest gossip, who is the most popular, who has the bigger paycheck, who has the better grades, who drives the nicest car, who wears the pricier clothes—the list goes on and on. And generally speaking, I tend to see a lot of female competition devoted to the issue of male attention or beauty. These tend to be particular areas of weakness (probably because these two issues are very close to a woman's heart). But competition can even be about matters that are much more trivial than these! Just think of little kids. They can compete over whose dollhouse has the most accessories, or who can hold her breath the longest. If you watch them long enough, you start to get the picture that often it's more about the competition itself than the actual prize. Humans tend to have this inborn desire to out-perform others, and more often than not, the things adults do are the same things children do, just on a more sophisticated level. If there is a contest and status involved, it's competition, and it doesn't matter what it is about.

Competition, sadly, doesn't exclude the topic of our spiritual life either. Unfortunately, women can compete about this area just like we compete about other things. That can mean competing over who knows more Scripture, who's been saved longer, whose Bible study attracts more people, who's closer to the pastor, who's more anointed, who's involved in the most ministries—anything. Ironically, competition itself is a worldly activity, as opposed to a "spiritual" one.

HOW DO WE COMPETE?

Competition comes in many forms. Sometimes we compete loudly, other times we compete silently. Sometimes it is obvious. Sometimes it lurks beneath the surface of social encounters. Either way, there is no denying its existence. We compete outwardly against other women, and we can also compete inwardly on our own private game board that nobody knows about. Let's identify some of the masks competition wears so we can identify places where it may threaten to pop up in our lives.

Boasting and Flaunting

Back to the game board analogy, sometimes women compete by flaunting their strengths or boasting about themselves. It's equivalent to moving their game pieces ahead a few spaces. I'll never forget, once I was out with a group of friends, and was particularly excited because I was going to get to see a guy, Devin, whom I had a huge crush on. In fact, my girls and I would talk about whom we each liked rather frequently. This evening, I pulled up outside of Devin's apartment where we were meeting, and one of my girlfriends, who had gotten there earlier, came up to me smiling and laughing. Then she looked at me and, giggling, said, "Oh Devin—he is such a flirt! I walked past him and he just told me how gorgeous I was!" Then she walked away. It was so confusing and hurtful, particularly since she had major feelings for another guy. True, no girl wants to hear that her crush complimented someone else. But my friend's words and laughter had some tinge to them, like she was trying to rub something in my face.

Dethroning the Queen

I felt like she was flaunting his attention. Women can be skilled at this—boasting just enough to scoot that little game piece ahead a couple spaces in the race to outdo the other woman. It's a major form of competition between women.

Criticizing

Another way a woman can compete is by using her biggest weapon: her tongue. Criticism is a particularly popular form of word-based competition. A woman walks in the door wearing a beautiful dress and another woman remarks that her shoes are the wrong color. It's like trying to move an opponent's game piece back a few spaces. One woman does something well, and her piece advances. Then to counteract her progress, another woman swiftly cuts her down with a corrective word and moves that game piece back. It's an attack, not an attempt to improve or help the criticized person. This type of criticism is mean-spirited or bitter, and is often used in competition.

Criticism-competition can also be achieved with slights and underhanded comments. These are the remarks that appear harmless, but have a cutting or hurtful undertone that the speaker is aware of. We will talk more about this concept of "subtext" in chapter eleven, but it is very prevalent in Queen Bee speech and can be used in competition.

Withholding Compliments

Women can also compete without using any words at all. Many women who struggle either consciously or subconsciously with competition will fail to compliment other women, most especially women they find threatening. Have you ever seen that happen? Sandra says, "Rachel, you look amazing," and Erin just stiffens and doesn't say anything. This form of competition is very passive. It's doing anything you possibly can to keep from having to help your opponent move forward in your game. That's a form of competition. Here's another thing I've seen—some women will give a general statement in place of a compliment. It's the same thing. For instance, Ericka gets a brand new hairdo for the upcoming party, and all Karen can say is, "You got a new hairdo?" or "Decided to change your hair, huh?" Or she'll make her compliment plural, "Everyone is really going all out for this party!" It's not that these statements are necessarily rooted in competition, for it's possible that perhaps Karen doesn't like the hairstyle and is trying to acknowledge it without having to give an opinion. But when a woman is extremely tight-lipped or reluctant when it comes to giving an actual compliment to a specific person, it's a very strong indicator that there is some sort of competition or other insecurity going on.

We don't have the ability to judge other people's motives, but we can judge our own. If you have ever experienced this, you know whether or not your compliment stinginess is out of competition!

Mirroring

One other way women can sometimes compete is by constantly mirroring somebody else's actions. April starts a business; Bianca starts a business. April gets a haircut; Bianca gets a new style. April starts writing poetry; Bianca starts writing, too. Bianca can do exactly what April does, or she can do her own rendition of what April does. Either type of behavior can characterize competition. Sometimes mirroring behavior is a mere result of admiration or inspiration. But sometimes it's a woman's way of competing. It's like trying to keep the other person from getting ahead. I think of this form of competition as a game of checkers—one of those games where one person keeps mirroring the exact moves of her opponent on her side of the board. It's annoying—it keeps the game from progressing. This mirroring behavior can be a form of competition. But again, since you don't know other women's motives, you can only judge your own behavior. It is for you to allow the Holy Spirit to reveal the intentions behind your actions.

THE PURPOSE OF DESCRIBING COMPETITION: SELF-EVALUATION

I want to make sure I emphasize the concept of self-evaluation. Pointing out ways competition happens is intended to foster honesty about the unspoken realities of many women's relationships. However, it is not a tool for group analysis. People are not equipped to make assumptions about someone else's motives. Now, if you feel uncomfortable about a particular woman, you have every right to decide how you let her into your life. But, it is critical that you do not use this information to point fingers—I guarantee finger pointing will always end up pointing back at you! Instead, focus more on your thoughts, your actions, and your heart. Whether you have been guilty of competition, have mastered it, or have never really dealt with it, focusing on self will always produce a better, more righteous result than focusing on others.

WHY DO WE COMPETE?

There are several reasons why women can begin competing with each other. While each person is different and the motives of one woman's heart are different from those of the next woman, there are some general principles about competition that provide useful insight into understanding what can cause it.

A Deep Lack

Competition usually hints at a deep sense of lack. Leah is a clear example. She did not keep getting pregnant because of her desire for many children. She was striving for something else—the love of her husband. Her speech says it all, for after her first son was born, she said, "Surely my husband will love me now," and after her third she said, "Now at last my husband will become attached to me, because I have borne him three sons" (Genesis 29:32b, 34). Leah had a deep desire for her husband's affection, and that is what fueled this competition, not a desire for many children.

The Queen of Competition

Often, competition happens the same way with us. We compete in one area of our lives to make up for the deep sense of lack we feel in another area.

Self-worth is a particularly major issue. This type of deep lack becomes a major insecurity. A woman who struggles with feeling valuable may be tempted to compete with another woman, hoping to gain some status that will validate her worth. For instance, she may begin to compete about looks, money, or male attention out of a deeper desire to compensate for her low self-esteem. But striving to exceed others in order to feel self-worth is a Queen Bee mentality. True royalty, on the other hand, does not need to prove itself. But when one is not surrendered to God, these areas of lack can drive women into highly competitive relationships.

Pride

Another much simpler reason for competition is pure, fleshly pride. As I mentioned earlier, there seems to be an inborn human need to out-perform others. We will go into pride in more detail in chapter twelve, but pride is a natural characteristic of the flesh. It always seeks self-glorification. Pride often drives people to compete with others out of a desire for praise.

Ignorance

Sometimes as women we compete just because we don't know better. Competition with other women is all we've ever seen, done, or been taught. Older sisters and friends have encouraged us to flaunt our strengths in front of other women, or to fight with women to get what we want. Competition is mistakenly viewed as being strong, self-protecting, or confident. In this case, it's ignorance that leads to competition.

Immaturity

Unfortunately, competition can also be a byproduct of immaturity. When a person needs to surpass someone else in order to feel validated or satisfied, they reflect a deficit in character. Reliance on competition shows that some inward condition is not fully developed. Greater maturity brings along with it a better understanding of self and others. Greater maturity also brings a more developed character—one that seeks not to exalt self over others, but to benefit and uplift others.

Searching for Purpose

Sometimes women also compete because we don't have our own sense of personal direction. I've seen this happen countless times. Someone starts getting involved in all the same activities and groups that someone else is involved in because it gives her a sense of meaning that she would otherwise lack. Many women who struggle with identifying their own goals tend to glean a sense of purpose from achieving other people's goals. These relationships can also become competitive.

Getting Caught Up

This is one dangerous phenomenon that happens fairly often between women—one woman starts competing because she is responding to the rivalry another woman initiated. Notice Leah does this with Rachel. By the time Leah had given birth to her fourth son, I believe she had reached a place of contentment in God. That's why she named him Judah, saying, "This time, I will praise the Lord" (Genesis 29:35b). But Rachel got jealous of Leah, and so she gave Jacob her maidservant to bear children. As soon as jealous Rachel got a family of her own to compete with Leah's, Leah started competing and striving again, and gave her maidservant to Jacob. When you take your eyes off of God and what He is doing in your own life, and start responding to somebody else's hang-ups, it's easy to get caught up in competition.

The Queen of Competition

THE PROBLEMS WITH COMPETITION

It's Futile

Did Leah's having more children than Rachel win Jacob's love? Did Rachel's womb open because she struggled against her sister? Of course not. That is a critical trap of competition—it only creates futile striving. Sometimes competing makes us feel as though we are achieving something, but competition never gets at the root of our sense of lack or need for validation. Striving is human effort. It exhausts one's energy, and often to no avail. It only produces more cycles of competition. Think of Rachel and Leah. God answered each of their prayers, but they sowed havoc into their own lives by engaging in competition—which only resulted in strife. Have you ever felt that way—striving to achieve something even though deep down you knew you couldn't make it happen on your own? Let me save you some time, energy, and drama. Competition will never give you what you're really looking for, and will only bring strife into your life. It's a lose-lose situation. It's like what God says in Jeremiah 2:13: "They have forsaken me, the spring of living water, and have dug their own cisterns, broken cisterns that cannot hold water." Competing against other women is like that—forfeiting what could be freely yours in a vain attempt to take it from another source.

Distracts from the Will of God

As mentioned earlier, Leah had reached a place of contentment in God by the time she had her fourth son, Judah. But competing took her out of that place. It took her eyes off of God, and removed her from a mindset of praise. It distracted her away from the very source of her blessings. Competition will distract you from the will of God. It requires expending a lot of energy watching and responding to other people, which will prevent you from watching and responding to God—often to your detriment.

Dethroning the Queen

Negatively Affects Others

I cannot ignore the fact that Rachel named her servant's second boy Naphtali. The footnote to that particular verse indicates the name means "my struggle" (Genesis 30:8). It's as if Rachel imposed her issues on her child, making them part of his very identity. Whenever I would read this story, I thought Naphtali was named so unfairly. Sometimes engaging in competition keeps us from being able to give healthily in our other relationships because we are so knee-deep in bitterness and rivalry. Those kinds of issues will always have some negative affect on a woman's loved ones!

Can Lead to Desperation

As we've also discussed earlier, competition is a form of striving—it's a vigorous attempt to gain something with one's own strength or effort. It's exhausting, and only sends the woman home frustrated and empty-handed. For many women, once they get to that point of exhaustion, they are so determined to get what they want that they become desperate. Leah is a very tragic example of that kind of desperation. In order to win some intimate time with Jacob, she resorted to hiring him, her own husband, with mandrake roots! For me, this is the saddest part of the story. The word "hired" always disturbed me, because it's a word used in prostitution (Genesis 30:16). Leah was not exactly prostituting herself, yet she resorted to the same degrading level of forced intimacy that characterizes prostitution. That's another part of why competition is dangerous—it can lead to increasingly desperate acts that compromise a woman's dignity and self-respect.

Competition Driven by Pride is Sin

When we struggle with competition purely out of a fleshly desire to be cuter, better, smarter, or cooler than somebody else, it's just sin. Paul commands us to, "Do nothing out of selfish ambition or vain conceit"

(Philippians. 2:3). But we will talk more about how and why pride is sinful in chapter twelve!

Sisters Become the Foe

We have touched on a few issues that make competition a problem: it's futile, it distracts us from God by making us focus too much on people, it negatively affects others, it leads to desperation, and it's sinful. But there is one more major problem with competition that we should know of, and perhaps it's the most important one. Competition turns your sisters into your foes. This aspect of competition is by far the most dangerous. Rachel and Leah were blood sisters turned rivals. Competition also turns friend against friend. It leads to division. As we discussed in chapter two, when we are divided, we forfeit the power of solidarity and cancerously fragment the body of Christ. We lose what even those chimpanzees had. Viewing our sisters as foes promotes ungodly attitudes toward other sisters in Christ, attitudes that could bring judgment upon us.

The thought that our sisters are the foes is a lie. Genesis 30:1 says, "When Rachel saw that she was not bearing Jacob any children, she became jealous of her sister." Competition is deceptive. Leah's having children had nothing to do with Rachel's barrenness. Yet, competition will mistakenly make the other woman out to be the enemy. She becomes the scapegoat for your hang-ups. As women of God, we do have a real foe—and that is Satan. But sometimes our real foe goes unopposed because we are too busy warring with our own soldiers. Competition skews our perspective and gives us a very unhealthy attitude toward both our sisters and Satan.

A GODLY EXAMPLE

We've seen Rachel and Leah's story. They represent a picture of what not to do. Now let's turn our attention to a godly example.

Dethroning the Queen

In the sixth month, God sent the angel Gabriel to Nazareth, a town in Galilee, to a virgin pledged to be married to a man named Joseph, a descendant of David. The virgin's name was Mary. The angel went to her and said, "Greetings, you who are highly favored! The Lord is with you." Mary was greatly troubled at his words and wondered what kind of greeting this might be. But the angel said to her, "Do not be afraid, Mary, you have found favor with God. You will be with child and give birth to a son, and you are to give him the name Jesus. He will be great and will be called the Son of the Most High. The Lord God will give him the throne of his father David, and he will reign over the house of Jacob forever; his kingdom will never end." "How will this be," Mary asked the angel, "since I am a virgin?" The angel answered, "The Holy Spirit will come upon you, and the power of the Most High will overshadow you. So the holy one to be born will be called the Son of God. Even Elizabeth your relative is going to have a child in her old age, and she who was said to be barren is in her sixth month. For nothing is impossible with God." "I am the Lord's servant," Mary answered. "May it be to me as you have said." Then the angel left her.

At that time Mary got ready and hurried to a town in the hill country of Judea, where she entered Zechariah's home and greeted Elizabeth. When Elizabeth heard Mary's greeting, the baby leaped in her womb, and Elizabeth was filled with the Holy Spirit. In a loud voice she exclaimed: "Blessed are you among women, and blessed is the child you will bear! But why am I so favored, that the mother of my Lord should come to me? As soon as the sound of your greeting reached my ears, the baby in my womb leaped for joy. Blessed is she who has believed that what the Lord has said to her will be accomplished!" (Luke 1:26–45).

The Queen of Competition

Both pairs of women are relatives, and women of God. Rachel and Leah were sisters, and Elizabeth and Mary were cousins, but their relationships are completely opposite. Rachel and Leah had an extremely competitive relationship, but Elizabeth and Mary did not. Instead, their relationship was characterized by rejoicing for each other. Let's look at their story for some points to emulate in our own relationships:

Practice Joyfulness

Elizabeth's response to Mary's news was extreme joyfulness, both emotionally and spiritually. Think about it—here's Elizabeth, a woman who's been disgraced before the other women because of her failure to have children. Then, in her old age, the Lord opens her womb to make way for John the Baptist (who would be her son). Some women in Elizabeth's position would have been soaking up as much attention as possible. But when the news about Mary came to Elizabeth, she was not upset that Mary was taking her spotlight (as I suspect some of us might have been). She wasn't upset that Mary had seen an angel, too, and also wasn't upset that Mary's pregnancy was divine. These are all things that would have totally stolen a carnal woman's thunder. It would have moved Mary's game piece up ahead of her own. But Elizabeth did not care. Instead she reacted to Mary's favor as if it had been bestowed on herself. This is the type of relationship we are called to have with other women in the Kingdom, for the Bible calls us to, "Rejoice with those who rejoice" (Romans 12:15).

Accept What's Yours

Mary also accepted her lot in life. Her response to the angel's message was, "May it be to me as you have said" (Luke 1:38). Ladies, in order to stop competing, it is critical to accept your lot in life—your body type, your form of beauty, your strengths, your destiny, your talents, your calling. Accepting yourself and your life will create a mindset of greater contentment. It takes away the need to strive for something else, and will help combat competition. When you are personally satisfied and content, there is no need to compete. It is better to accept what the Lord has given you than to tire yourself out competing for something that is not yours to begin with.

Think About What's Yours

Not only did Mary accept what was hers, but she practiced thinking about what was hers as well. Several times, as in Luke 2:19, the Bible says, "Mary treasured up all these things and pondered them in her heart." When you practice meditating and reflecting on what's going on in your own life, you are not as easily tempted to fixate on what is going on in other people's lives. Thinking about what is yours can play a big part in diminishing competition.

Realize There's Room for All

Both Mary and Elizabeth have amazing stories—and one woman's story does not make the other woman's story less amazing! Proverbs 18:16a says, "A man's gift makes room for him" (NASB). There is room for all who have something to offer to this world. There are never too many anointed women, too many teachers, too many servants, too many ministers, too many mothers, too many wives. There is room for them all.

This is especially true in ministry. In Matthew 9:37, Jesus says, "The harvest is plentiful but the workers are few," and encourages His disciples to pray for more ministers to do all the work they'd been called to do! Don't get bent out of shape if you're writing a book, and another woman starts writing a book, too! She's just helping to lift the load, because you can't possibly do it all yourself. Real estate agents compete over listings because there are more agents than listings. Not so in the Kingdom! There is plenty of work to go around—especially with regard to spiritual territory. We, as the kingdom of God, will be held accountable for the work we've done, so let other ministers help you make some progress!

Life in Christ is not a game of musical chairs. There is a seat for your

The Queen of Competition

gift and your blessings. Psalms 139 says, "All the days ordained for me were written in your book before one of them came to be" (Psalms 139:16). Ephesians 2:10 says we were "created in Christ Jesus to do good works, which God prepared in advance for us to do." When God calls us to do something, or ordains a blessing for our lives, He makes a seat for us. It's like a table marked "Reserved" that is waiting for us before we get there! So it doesn't matter if Suzy tries to race to the room first, because when she gets there she will see a sign marked "Reserved for Alicia Renee Sheppard." No competing woman has the power to rewrite what the Lord has written in His book concerning you, so don't even bother competing back. If you are obedient and faithful, God will grant you everything He has for you! Nobody can beat you to the top, and you won't need to beat anyone else to the top—just get there yourself.

Given the points above, here is another point—if you're in a situation where you have to compete, rethink things. God does not play musical chairs. For instance, if you have to compete for a man, rethink whether or not he's really for you. If he is, he'll come for you no matter how many women hang off him, and you'll get him without having to subject yourself to degradation. On the other hand, if he doesn't come—there's your answer! Either he's not for you or he's not good enough for you! If you're trying to lead Bible study and somebody else is trying to lead the same one, rethink things! Either you're supposed to work together (like the disciples) or one of you needs to find her own work to do.

Just remember, there is no need to compete; there is room for every woman to get everything God has for her. There needed to be both a Jesus and a John the Baptist. Therefore, there needed to be both a Mary and an Elizabeth.

On the Same Team

Ultimately, it is most important to remember—your sisters are made to be on your team! Competition, then, becomes a contradiction. Remember what we discussed in chapter two; we are all one body. We need each other to function. 1 Corinthians 12:26 says, "If one part suffers, every part suffers with it; if one part is honored, every part rejoices with it." In the kingdom of God, a sister's victory is your victory, and vice versa. Our success is tied to other women in the body. For instance, Elizabeth and Mary's stories were interdependent. John the Baptist prepared the way for Jesus! Competition between the two women would have been harmful to each one. If you are competing with your sister, you may be persecuting the counterpart to your own blessing! Remember that your sisters in Christ are on your team!

A Prize Worth Fighting For

Finally, consider this: if you are fighting so desperately for something in this world that you are competing with your sisters, how are your priorities? In Matthew 6:19–21, Jesus says, "Do not store up for yourselves treasures on earth, where moth and rust destroy, and where thieves break in and steal. But store up for yourselves treasures in heaven, where moth and rust do not destroy, and where thieves do not break in and steal. For where your treasure is, there your heart will be also." If you are competing, you should probably check your heart. Chances are, you are putting too much emphasis on earthly things and should ask the Lord to give you a greater desire for heavenly treasures. Desiring heavenly treasure involves desiring things like righteousness, godliness, and love—which will discourage the tendency toward competition.

ONE LAST LOOK AT RACHEL AND LEAH

As we conclude this chapter, think about Rachel and Leah's story, and decide instead to give your unmet desires to the Lord. It was God who opened both Rachel and Leah's wombs. It was He who heard their cries and responded. Instead of looking at other women, look at God and give your requests to Him. He is the One who can help you. Matthew 6:33 says, "But

The Queen of Competition

seek first his kingdom and his righteousness, and all these things will be given to you as well." These things will be added to you, but first, your heart and focus need to be on God's Kingdom. On His Kingdom—that includes the body of Christ. How can you ask God for what you want when you are sowing division into the Kingdom by competing with your sisters in Christ? Instead, dethrone the Queen of Competition and rest in the fact that God hears you and is able to lovingly provide for you—you will have no need to compete with your sisters when you do!

Prayer

Dear Lord,

Thank You for Your Word, which brings truth, correction, and direction. I pray now that You would help me to stop competing with other women. Please forgive me for the sinful attitude and action of competition, especially toward_____. Please renew my mind about competition and give me a deep understanding that my sisters are not my enemies. Give me an understanding of my unique attributes, achievements, and callings that were prepared just for me to do, so that I am not tempted to wrestle against other women when I look at their lives. Help me to see that all competition is in vain, and that You are my source. Show me, in an even more profound way, my worth, and my royalty, so I am not tempted to prove myself by outdoing others. Show me my overt behavior, my subtle speech, or my secret thoughts that come from a heart or motive of competition. Then, dethrone the Queen of Competition in my heart, and help me to start rejoicing with my sisters in Christ and appreciating what I have. I thank You for already beginning to do it! In Jesus' Name, I pray. Amen.

Memory Verse

"If one part suffers, every part suffers with it; if one part is honored, every part rejoices with it."
1 CORINTHIANS 12:26

Dethroning the Queen

Reflection Questions

What are the things that you strive for on a daily basis? What does your heart really want?

Do you compete? Whom do you compete against?

How do you compete?

What (or who) makes you feel threatened?

What do you use as your "offense" when you compete? (i.e. I flaunt my looks when I feel threatened about my personality, etc.)

Who and what is suffering as a result of your competition?

Is there an insecurity in you that tempts you to compete? If so, what is it? Are you ready to give it to God?

Action Plan!

Write a journal entry about the desires and insecurities that drive you to compete. Include a prayer, giving these issues over to God. Note those women whom you want to change your attitude toward, and track your progress. Pray for a heart to compliment them and be happy for them.

CHAPTER FIVE

The Queen of Jealousy

"You are still worldly. For since there is jealousy and quarreling among you, are you not worldly?"
1 CORINTHIANS 3:3

I THINK OF MY SKIN CRAWLING when I saw a girl getting a piggyback ride from a guy I really liked. I think of my best friend in elementary school walking into my freshly made-up bedroom full of games and toys, and being silent for five whole minutes. (It took a few days for her to finally say she was upset because my room "had everything she ever wanted"). I think of the woman who worked diligently on her research project only to look in dismay upon the other woman whose project earned a higher score. I think of the woman who gets angry at women who even sit on the couch next to the man she likes. I think of walking into the room with a brand new dress and seeing the backs of other women instantly stiffen. (That stiffening effect is out of control and I think most of us have probably experienced it—we definitely need to get over that one!)

Yes, it's the most notorious Queen Bee of them all—Queen Jealousy! And she is a nasty one!

DEFINING JEALOUSY

The New International Webster's Concise Dictionary defines the word jealousy this way:

Dethroning the Queen

1. "Suspicious and resentful of a rival or of rivalry in general."
2. "Hostile or envious over the advantages, good fortune, etc. of others.
3. "Earnestly vigilant in guarding or keeping something."[1]

Now, there are two types of jealousy. The first kind is most adequately summed up in definition two. That kind of jealousy is about desiring and being upset about what other people have. This type of jealousy is more accurately called "envy." The second type of jealousy is the kind you encounter in the Bible wherever you see God refer to Himself as a "Jealous God" (Exodus 20:5). This type of jealousy is best summed up in definition three. It has to do with a sense of ownership, and taking great care into seeing that nothing rightfully belonging to oneself is taken by another. This definition of jealousy is most accurate, but often in general conversation, people use jealousy and envy interchangeably. They are not the same, though they can be related. Just remember, a very simple way of distinguishing between the two is this—envy is about something you don't own, and jealousy is about something you do own. But for all practical purposes, in this chapter we will mostly refer to it all as "jealousy."

So, to round out our definition of jealousy, let's also look at the definition of *envy:*

1. "A feeling of resentment and jealousy over the possessions, achievements, etc., of another."
2. "Desire for something belonging to another."[2]

In this chapter, we will deal with the whole shebang. Desiring something that belongs to someone else, being resentful about the advantages belonging to someone else, guarding something you feel entitled to—we'll talk about it all in this chapter devoted to exposing and dethroning Queen Jealousy!

The Queen of Jealousy

SOME BASIC PROBLEMS WITH JEALOUSY

Dysfunctional Sisterhood

There are some basic problems with jealousy. First, it's contrary to the nature of the body of believers. We have been talking in the previous few chapters about how we are the body of Christ and are called to be united. Jealousy, on the other hand, often contains an element of suspicion. For example, a jealous girlfriend is suspicious of other women. It expects wrong in others when we should expect goodness, holiness, righteousness, etc. Now sadly, that expectation is not always unfounded, for there are many people in this world whose character is dubious. But, suspicion certainly is not God's design for us, so jealousy is problematic. Furthermore, like competition, jealousy involves considering others as rivals. We saw this kind of rivalry between Rachel and Leah in chapter four. They were sisters who were jealous of each other, and so they became bitter rivals. Another big problem with jealousy is it fosters resentment. Most of us know the feeling. But the people of God, on the other hand, are called to "Rejoice with those who rejoice" (Romans 12:15). All of these problems with jealousy (suspicion, rivalry, resentment) contribute to dysfunctional sisterhood, which is one of the main problems we are looking to address in this book. Women can't get along if they are bitter about other women's fortunes.

Personal Limitations

The other major issue we want to address in this book is how relational issues with other women can hinder not just our relationships, but also ourselves as individuals. One way is by causing us to have contempt for what we have, or to take what we have for granted. If you spend all your time being jealous about somebody else's life, when is there ever time for you to enjoy your own? It's like the old saying, "The grass is always greener on the other side of the fence." Jealousy makes you think what other people have is better than what you have and creates a perpetual state of discontentment or ingratitude.

Another way jealousy harms us is by causing us to stray from purpose. When we are focused on our own gifts and talents, we are able to put them into good use and walk in the will of God for our lives. Ephesians 2:10 reminds us, "We are God's workmanship, created in Christ Jesus to do good works, which God prepared in advance for us to do." God's Word repeatedly assures us that there is a specific plan and purpose for each of our lives, and I believe that only when we walk in our God-given plan will we be truly happy and fulfilled. Jealousy can hinder us from living purposeful, fulfilling, God-glorifying lives by causing us to look at and covet other people's gifts, which almost inevitably causes us to despise or undermine our own gifts and talents, if not overlook them altogether! In a way, jealousy is like a sister to comparison, except jealousy has tunnel vision— it focuses almost solely on what others have.

In Matthew 25:14–30, Jesus tells the parable of the talents. Jesus told this story to emphasize the importance of being faithful over that which God has given us. The parable demonstrates how God rewards and approves of those who are faithful, but is displeased with those who fail to complete His assignments. Jealousy severely hinders our ability to get a full return on our Master's "talents," thus putting us in the dangerous position of displeasing Him. How can we be faithful over what we have when we are jealous of what other people have?

In short, jealousy distracts us from our own lives and even our purpose. It can cause us to desire other things so much that we place a lesser value on what we have, or fail to use those things for God's glory. An even deeper problem with jealousy is the kind of heart that accompanies it. This is probably the most detrimental issue with jealousy, but we will discuss the heart later on in this chapter.

The Queen of Jealousy

Insight into Women and Jealousy

I am sure we can all think of endless instances where a woman was jealous. Jealousy is a far-reaching issue, and there are many reasons why women can be jealous. But I believe there is a fundamental revelation about the cause of jealousy found in James 4:1–3: "What causes fights and quarrels among you? Don't they come from your desires that battle within you? You want something but don't get it. You kill and covet, but you cannot have what you want. You quarrel and fight. You do not have, because you do not ask God. When you ask, you do not receive, because you ask with wrong motives, that you may spend what you get on your pleasures."

There are several enlightening principles about jealousy found in this passage—let's take a look at what they are. The real reason some of us don't get along is because we're jealous. Ever hear women talk about the people they dislike? Sometimes it doesn't even make sense. I've heard women say things like, "I don't know, it's just something about the way she walks," or "I don't like how she's new and all of a sudden she's talking to everybody." If you haven't heard these kind of odd comments, you're probably thinking, "Who would say that?" Well, many women do. Sometimes women claim to dislike other women for trivial or even seemingly credible reasons, but often the case is the person is just jealous! Notice in verse one James says "fights and quarrels" come from "desires that battle within you." "Desires that battle" speaks of envy. It speaks of wanting something that belongs to someone else, and warring with that person by considering him or her a rival. When someone can't articulate a good reason for disliking someone, it's quite probable the person is just jealous. This passage makes it clear that often unknown sources of anger between individuals can be traced to jealousy.

Jealousy only leads to frustration (being kept from something we want). James repeatedly mentions people not getting what they want in this passage. That is the essence of frustration: the state of being blocked from something you want. Well, jealousy leads to frustration. When you stare at the green grass in someone else's yard, you come very close to the fence. When you spend your time desiring what belongs to others, you inevitably run smack dab into the obstacles that keep you from having what you want. For instance, if you're in love with a married man, you will constantly be faced with the fact that he is married! Jealousy brings people close to barriers, and thus becomes a breeding ground for frustration.

Jealousy is our own frustration pointed at somebody else. Notice verse two says, "You kill and covet." These are actions based on frustration. You sense you are being kept from what you want, so you seek some sort of redemptive action. You take the matter in your own hands. For instance, Joseph's brothers were frustrated because they did not have the special attention Joseph received. Unable to get that special attention, they directed their frustration at Joseph by trying to kill him. Joseph wasn't really the problem, but they tried to kill him nonetheless. Jealousy isn't always rational. It often takes out its aggression on other people, which only produces more frustration by failing to solve the problem.

We're jealous basically because we don't have what we want! James clarifies this point. A woman is not jealous because of the other woman. A woman is jealous because of her unmet desires. That desire could be for a man, for attention, for love, for prestige—anything—but the root cause of jealousy is that inner desire, not the other people. Again, consider Rachel and Leah from chapter four. Genesis 30:1 says, "When Rachel saw that she was not bearing Jacob any children, she became jealous of her sister." This jealousy launched a massive competitive rivalry between the two sisters. But the truth was Rachel's jealousy had nothing to do with Leah, and everything to do with her own unmet desire to be a mother. Jealousy is about you, not the other person.

One reason we probably don't have our way is because we have not

The Queen of Jealousy

asked God. Being jealous doesn't solve problems. God solves problems. But too often, we don't wait for God's hand (which is essentially ceasing to ask Him). Instead, we take matters into our own hands and strive for what we want with our own strength. Circumventing God is a great way to not get what you want, as James makes very clear! There may be many reasons why someone fails to ask God, such as impatience, lack of faith, or lack of submission to God's will. Matthew 6:33 says, "But seek first his kingdom and his righteousness, and all these things will be given to you as well," but many people are unwilling to do that. Instead, they resort to their own measures.

Or, we don't have what we want because our motives are wrong. 1 John 5:14 says, "This is the confidence we have in approaching God: that if we ask anything according to his will, he hears us." How can we pray for something when our motives are wrong and we are not surrendered to God's will? It is sinful to be jealous! In fact, that is one of the Ten Commandments: "You shall not covet" (Exodus 20:17). When our desires are not God's desires, we run the risk of not getting what we want (which is actually merciful on God's part)! If you are struggling with a feeling of jealousy, check the motive behind your desires!

These are some insights into how and why we become jealous. Now, let's gain some insight into the most important aspect of jealousy: the heart condition.

THE HEART OF JEALOUSY

Whenever you see jealousy occurring in the Bible, it's very clear that there is a deeper heart condition behind the surface actions of a jealous person. Having a heart of jealousy is like having a heart full of poison. The bitterness and resentment jealousy fosters is toxic. Jealousy is most dangerous because of what happens in the heart when we are jealous. In order to dethrone Queen Jealousy, let's take a deeper look at the heart of a jealous person.

Dethroning the Queen

A MURDEROUS OR HATEFUL HEART

Cain and Abel

The first time we see jealousy clearly in the Bible is in the first family God created! Genesis 4 tells the story. Adam and Eve's first son Cain worked the soil, and Abel, their younger son, kept flocks. As an offering, Cain gave the Lord some fruit from the soil, but Abel brought some of the best of the firstborn of his flock. Essentially, Abel gave an offering out of the best of what he had, while Cain seemed to only give a mediocre offering to the Lord. Thus, God looked with favor on Abel's offering and not on Cain's. For that reason, Cain became angry and killed his brother Abel. As punishment, God made Cain a wanderer on the earth who would no longer be able to yield crops from the ground.

Cain resented the Lord's favor on Abel's offering so much that he killed his own brother! Isn't that the essence of jealousy? We become resentful of a good thing in someone else's life because we don't have that thing in our lives, and as we can see, that kind of resentment can lead to murder! That is why Jesus placed so much emphasis on our hearts, because he knew: "The good man brings good things out of the good stored up in him, but the evil man brings evil things out of the evil stored up in him" (Matthew 12:35). When there is evil in our hearts, evil actions follow.

1 John 3:15 says, "Anyone who hates his brother is a murderer." Jealousy is like hatred. It contains the same traces of deep resentment, and as the Scripture says, a hateful, jealous heart is the same as a murderous heart. In fact, throughout history there have been quite a few celebrities and public figures who have been murdered by jealous associates. Or consider first-born children when the second child is born. The older is used to getting all the attention. Haven't you heard of those children who will bite, scratch, or even sit on the newborn infant? Jealousy is violent. Now I am not saying that if a person struggles with jealousy then she is at risk of committing some sort of violent crime. But understand that a person

The Queen of Jealousy

who struggles with jealousy might have the same hateful heart as a murderer. God always looks at the heart, after all, "it is the wellspring of life" (Proverbs 4:23b)—and jealousy indicates a major heart problem.

Joseph and His Brothers

Cain and Abel are not the only people whose jealousy led to murder. Joseph's brothers also struggled with a murderous jealousy. Genesis 37 tells the story of how Joseph, Jacob's favorite and youngest of twelve sons, was hated by his brothers. Verse four says, "When his brothers saw that their father loved him more than any of them, they hated him and could not speak a kind word to him." Similar to Cain, Joseph's brothers attempted to actually murder him because of their intense jealousy. One day when Joseph was walking out to meet his brothers, they said to each other, "Here comes that dreamer!

…Come now, let's kill him and throw him into one of these cisterns and say that a ferocious animal devoured him. Then we'll see what comes of his dreams" (Genesis 37:19, 20). Can you imagine a jealousy so intense that a man would kill his own brother? Apparently, Cain and Joseph's brothers experienced that kind of jealousy. The brothers felt threatened by Joseph's dreams, which prophetically spoke of the day when Joseph would rule over his family as second-in-command to the King of Egypt, and because of those insecurities, they wanted to see Joseph's dreams killed, even if it meant killing Joseph himself! Once again, we see how jealousy, hatred, and murder are all linked at the root.

The Two Prostitutes

One more instance of murderous jealousy is in the story of the two prostitutes who came to see King Solomon. Both women lived in the same house and each had just given birth. During the night, one of the women accidentally killed her child by laying on it, so she put the dead baby next to the other woman and took the live baby for herself. In the morning, the woman lying next to the dead baby looked at the child and realized it wasn't hers. The two of them went to King Solomon, who was known for his great wisdom, disputing about which of them was the mother of the living baby. Solomon, in his wisdom, called for someone to bring him a sword. Then he said he would cut the living baby in two and give half to each mother. The real mother cried out and pleaded with Solomon not to kill the child and to let the other woman have him, saying, "Please, my lord, give her the living baby! Don't kill him!" But the other woman, who had accidentally killed her son and tried to replace him with the other baby, said, "Neither I nor you shall have him. Cut him in two!" (1 Kings 3:26b). Because Solomon was wise, he was able to realize the living baby belonged to the first woman who was willing to give up her child if that's what it took to keep him alive, versus the second woman who was willing to have the child killed.

In this instance, as in the stories of Cain and Joseph's brothers, jealousy created a capacity for murder. The childless prostitute did not only want to steal the other woman's infant, but she would rather neither of them have a child than for the other woman to have a child while she herself remained childless. That kind of behavior is very typical of jealousy—not only desiring what belongs to someone else, but not wanting anyone else to have it either. Even worse, as part of her jealousy, this woman even encouraged the murder of a baby!

All of these stories give us insight into how problematic jealousy is in our lives. Cain resented his brother's favor and right standing with God. Joseph's brothers resented how special Joseph was, with his dreams and extra attention from his father. The prostitute resented the fact that her baby died, and also resented that the other woman had a child. These are all different examples of jealousy, but all these stories demonstrate how jealousy has the potential to lead to acts as drastic as murder. There is something very dangerous and hateful at the root of jealousy. That's why we cannot ignore jealousy in our own lives. Even though, for most of us,

The Queen of Jealousy

jealousy does not lead to murder, we are still harboring the seed that has the power to produce its fruit. With this insight into the nature and gravity of jealousy, we are hopefully more motivated to eradicate it.

AN UNGRATEFUL HEART

Another dimension of jealousy is a heart of ingratitude. Sometimes when we are jealous, we focus so much on what we do not have that we fail to acknowledge what we do have. The Bible talks about people with this problem as well.

The Prodigal Son

When most people think of the story of the prodigal son, they think about the story of a young guy who rebelled against his father, squandered his father's wealth and inheritance on wild living, eventually fell flat on his face, and crawled back home, but was greeted with open arms and celebration instead of chastisement and scorn. It parallels the way God treats us when we sin. Not only does He forgive us, but He lavishes us with grace and celebrates our return. However, I always saw another, seldom mentioned aspect in this story. Whenever I read it, I am intrigued by the brother's reaction, probably because I have often identified with his struggle. When the brother saw that the prodigal son had returned and that the father had killed the fattened calf and was throwing a party in celebration, the Bible says, "The older brother became angry and refused to go in" (Luke 15:28a). His father came outside to see what was wrong and to plead with him, and the older brother responded, saying, "Look! All these years I've been slaving for you and never disobeyed your orders. Yet you never gave me even a young goat so I could celebrate with my friends. But when this son of yours who has squandered your property with prostitutes comes home, you kill the fattened calf for him!" (Luke 15:29, 30).

The father's response is very simple. He merely says, "My son, you are always with me, and everything I have is yours. But we had to celebrate and be glad, because this brother of yours was dead and is alive again; he was lost and is found" (Luke 15:31, 32).

For a long time I thought I understood why the brother was so upset. In his eyes, his younger brother was being rewarded despite his disobedience. But as for himself, he had been obedient and had faithfully worked for his father for years, yet no one was rewarding him, killing the fattened calf, or partying for him! His argument made a lot of sense to me for a long time, until the Lord revealed to me part of the older brother's problem. The older brother was focused on a single event—the party celebrating the younger son's return. But such fixation on what his brother received caused him to ignore all he already had. In verse thirty-one, the father says, "Everything I have is yours." Think about that for a moment. The father owns a large estate with many livestock and servants. Even his servants have plenty of food to eat. Clearly, the family is prosperous, and the father says his son shares in everything he owns. The older son probably could have had a party whenever he wanted to, and all the years that he's lived with his father he's been able to share in the estate. He is privy to all of his father's wealth. Yet, when he focuses in on the party, he forgets about the estate, wealth, and untapped inheritance. Focusing so much on what someone else has can lead us to act as if we do not have much greater things. In its essence, jealousy can very well become ingratitude.

IMPORTANCE OF THE HEART—PULLING OUT AT THE ROOT!

The heart is important because with jealousy, you can't just stop the action. Jealousy bears fruit in your thoughts and actions, but takes deep root in your heart, where it often intertwines with all sorts of other problems. So in order to understand jealousy, you've got to see what's going on in your heart. You've got to see to the roots. Again, I am not saying you are secretly plotting murder if you are jealous, but I am seriously saying that you must understand what a jealous heart really looks like. God sees our hearts, and whether you are like Cain or like the woman rolling her eyes at the new

The Queen of Jealousy

girl with a pretty dress, God will see: jealous heart. Jealousy is a deep spiritual issue. If you want to dethrone Queen Jealousy, you've got to cut it off from underneath the surface; you've got to fix your heart.

Have you ever had to pull weeds? When you pull weeds, you have to pull from the root so they won't grow back. I used to have to pull weeds out in our backyard as a kid when we first moved in to our new house. In order to do it, I had to wear thick gloves and get down low while pulling hard. If you just tug at the tip of the weed, only the top will snap off and the weed will keep growing underneath the ground. But when you get down low to pull, you feel something pulling under the ground, and it takes a lot of strength, but when you give it a big pull, a huge root comes up out of the ground. Well, that's how jealousy is. It doesn't matter if it ever yields murder—jealousy will bear bad fruit no matter what it looks like, and none of it is pleasing to God. It will keep growing unless you get at your heart.

DETECTING JEALOUSY

Now's the hard part! Begin to ask the Holy Spirit to reveal areas where you may be dealing with jealousy. If you struggle with jealousy, He will lovingly guide you through the process of overcoming it! Here are some signs of jealousy that may indicate a problem:

1. Can't give compliments. (Remember Joseph's brothers? Genesis 37:4 says, "When his brothers saw that their father loved him more than any of them, they hated him and could not speak a kind word to him.")
2. Find it hard to be happy for someone else.
3. Resentful of successes of others.
4. Ungrateful.
5. Competitive.
6. Not walking in purpose.

Dethroning the Queen

7. Focus much attention on what someone else has while feeling unsatisfied with what you have.

Nobody wants to admit they're jealous. Jealousy has always been a characteristic that I adamantly wanted to avoid or deny at all costs. I thought confessing I was jealous would mean confessing that someone was better than I was. It seemed to me that jealousy plagued people with low self-esteem. To me, admitting jealousy was like admitting inferiority.

Jealousy can be particularly embarrassing. Don't be ashamed! It's worse to remain jealous than to just admit it and get over it! You do not have to feel inferior, worthless, or inadequate simply because you wrestle with jealousy. The Bible tells us that, "All have sinned and fall short of the glory of God, and are justified freely by his grace through the redemption that came by Christ Jesus" (Romans 3:23, 24). Jealousy is a sin like all the other sins. We do not have to be ashamed of our sin, because God has already covered it with His blood. When we confess and repent, we are healed and cleansed of our impurities.

Furthermore, you can't hide it. Hiding sin in our hearts gives the illusion that the sin is gone, when really it is alive and well. Just like when seeds hidden under the ground grow and produce all sorts of plants, sin hidden under the surface of our hearts is given a warm place to grow, fester, and produce bad fruit in our lives. There was a time in my life when I tried to deny the fact that I was jealous, and looking back on it, the picture I see in my mind is of a woman trying to hide the seeds of jealousy in her heart while constantly trying to trim away and conceal all the leaves and branches that have grown out and around her, entangling her. Jealousy is obvious, if not to others (which it frequently is), then certainly to God, for Hebrews 4:13 says, "Nothing in all creation is hidden from God's sight. Everything is uncovered and laid bare before the eyes of him to whom we must give an account." But the good news is, there is no condemnation, for forgiveness comes with repentance, and we are justified by grace!

The Queen of Jealousy

The truth is that admitting jealousy is a ticket out of degradation, not a ticket into it. When Paul was talking to the Corinthians, he said, "Brothers, I could not address you as spiritual but as worldly—mere infants in Christ. I gave you milk, not solid food, for you were not yet ready for it. Indeed, you are still not ready. You are still worldly. For since there is jealousy and quarreling among you, are you not worldly?" (1 Corinthians 3:1–3). Clearly, if we want to be victorious women of God and arise from immaturity, we must dethrone Queen Jealousy. But doing so requires being honest with ourselves. Only after identifying and admitting jealousy can we remove it.

Don't be embarrassed! I think jealousy is one of the most well-known and talked about Queen Bee characteristics—if you struggle with it, you're certainly not alone! As you meditate on this chapter, pray the Holy Spirit, who disciplines those He loves according to Hebrews 12:6, reveals to you what He needs to reveal about you. He disciplines only with the intention of making us more like Him!

Starting the Process

1. If you wrestle with jealousy, the first thing to do is to acknowledge the sin of jealousy. First John 1:8 says, "If we claim to be without sin, we deceive ourselves and the truth is not in us." You may not struggle with jealousy, but if you do, it is important to acknowledge it. Who are you jealous of? What are you jealous about? What do you desire? What do you attempt to guard from others? Who in your life elicits feelings of resentment? These are questions to ask yourself as you acknowledge the problem.

2. Next, it is important to repent. First John 1:9 says, "If we confess our sins, he is faithful and just and will forgive us our sins and purify us from all unrighteousness." That means repentance brings both forgiveness and cleansing.

3. Ask the Lord to renew you. In Ezekiel 36:26, the Lord declares to Israel, "I will give you a new heart and put a new spirit in you; I will remove from you your heart of stone and give you a heart of flesh." It is that same regenerative aspect of the Lord that inspired David to pray, "Create in me a pure heart, O God, and renew a steadfast spirit within me" (Psalms 51:10). According to 1 Corinthians 5:17, when we accept Christ, we are a new creation! We have access to a new heart, a pure heart, and a heart of flesh, not stone. When we allow sin to creep back in, we can confidently ask God to purify and renew us, and He will do it!

4. Choose to walk in the Spirit. Walking in the Spirit is a constant choice. Colossians 3:5 says, "Put to death, therefore, whatever belongs to your earthly nature," which includes jealousy. Instead of walking in the flesh, walk in the Spirit. Galatians 5:16 says, "Live by the Spirit, and you will not gratify the desires of the sinful nature." Of course, walking in the Spirit is easier said than done, but it is a constant choice to live life under God's direction and stay in His presence in order to gain access to His divine power. As we walk in the Spirit, God begins to cut away our fleshly attitudes and desires, empowering us to be like Him. The less we'll sin, and the holier we'll become!

5. Give thanks! The Bible talks a lot about thanksgiving. When we open our mouths to give thanks to God, it encourages us to have grateful hearts, not covetous hearts. It's never a good idea to take any blessing for granted or to insult God by desiring what He's given to others. Spend energy showing appreciation to the Lord for what He's done for you, and you'll spend less energy being jealous of others.

6. Overcoming jealousy is not just about you and God, but it also involves others. One very important thing to do is learn to

rejoice with others! Start practicing it—give thanks to God for other women's blessings, share in their joy, and offer compliments and words of happiness. Let that practice seep into you and change your habits and mentalities. The Holy Spirit will help you to do this if you let Him.

7. Examine major areas of lack. This step is major. Insecurity drives much of women's fighting, as James 4:1–3 makes clear. If we weren't insecure, I do not think we would have problems getting along the way we do. So, in order to deal with jealousy, we have to deal with our insecurities and unmet desires. There are certain areas that seem to strike women very deeply, such as love, affirmation, and relationship. These areas tend to produce much jealousy because they are so ardently desired. You may not identify with a deep feeling of lack, or you may identify with a different area of lack other than the three mentioned here. In any case, it is important to go to God with your insecurities and desires. These are the areas that often create the worst character flaws. Spend time thinking about what your areas of lack might be, and present them to God in prayer. You may even want to seek out a close friend or prayer partner to help you examine these issues.

Prayer

Dear God,

Thank You for dying on the cross for my sins. Thank You that I do not have to be ashamed of my shortcomings, but rather I can give them to You and be cleansed. So Lord, I confess now that I have been jealous of other women and have had envy in my heart. Please forgive me and change my heart. I know how serious jealousy is, and I do not want my attitude toward other women to be hostile, nor do I want my attitude toward You to be ungrateful. Both attitudes are dangerous. Lord, please teach me contentment. Remind me to come to You with my desires, and not to spend time focusing on what other people have. Remove the toxic poison of resentment in my heart. Keep my eyes on You, and give me a heart of gratitude. Teach me how to rejoice with other women in my heart, and not be threatened by their blessings. And I present my desires to You right now, for You to examine, reveal, and handle according to Your will and Your goodness. And I ask Your Holy Spirit to walk with me through this process as I let You dethrone Queen Jealousy in my life. Lord, please make me more like You. Thank You for Your power and purifying Spirit. In Jesus' Name, I pray. Amen.

Memory Verses

"What causes fights and quarrels among you? Don't they come from your desires that battle within you? You want something but don't get it. You kill and covet, but you cannot have what you want. You quarrel and fight. You do not have, because you do not ask God. When you ask, you do not receive, because you ask with wrong motives, that you may spend what you get on your pleasures."
JAMES 4:1–3

"But seek first his kingdom and his righteousness, and all these things will be given to you as well."
MATTHEW 6:33

Reflection Questions

Do you ever find it difficult to speak kind words to another woman?

Is it hard to be happy for certain people?

The Queen of Jealousy

Do you ever find yourself experiencing feelings of resentment toward another woman? When do those feelings arise?

Which if any of the concepts in this chapter offered you the greatest insight into jealousy? Did you find anything alarming?

Who are you jealous of? Why?

What desires do you need to present to the Lord?

In what areas do you need to practice more thanksgiving?

Action Plan!

Start finding ways to compliment and rejoice with others (particularly those who elicit feelings of jealousy). Ask the Holy Spirit to guide you in ways of doing this.

Speak aloud or write down a prayer of thanksgiving to the Lord. Try to be especially detailed in areas where you have experienced jealousy or have become ungrateful or blind to the ways in which God has blessed you.

CHAPTER SIX

The Queen of Antipathy

*"Anyone who claims to be in the light but hates his brother
is still in the darkness."*

1 JOHN 2:9

SOMETIMES YOU JUST DON'T LIKE CERTAIN PEOPLE. That's really the essence of Queen Antipathy—it's not fancy or complex, it's just plain old dislike. In simple terms, she's Queen "I-Don't-Like-Her!" Let's define this concept of dislike. People have come to commonly make a distinction between loving someone and liking someone. First there's love, for which people have created many definitions. People often use the word love when they are talking about family, dear friends, spouses, or boyfriends. Love is often thought of as deep affection. It's also regarded as something permanent or unconditional. Some people shy away from the cultural definitions of love and stick to 1 Corinthians 13:4–7, which says, "Love is patient, love is kind. It does not envy, it does not boast." Selflessness. Self-sacrifice. Commitment. These are other words commonly associated with love. Many people also agree true love is not based on emotions. Now due to the fact that love is commonly defined this way, "liking" has developed into its own category. Liking has to do with preference and pleasure. It involves actually enjoying someone and wanting to be around that person. Because of this duplicity, I have heard people say things like, "I love her, but I don't like her." Take the example of annoying family members, for instance. You have to get along with them, you're there for them if they need you, if they're in a bind they can come to you, you care about their well-being, you are committed to them in some way, but at the end of the day, you don't "like" them. You find their presence or personality to be unpleasant. You do not prefer to be around them. You would not choose them as your company. Disliking people can often include having feelings of ill will or deep repulsion. Think of a woman you don't like. Fancy words can't really describe it. So some basic terms would be, "I can't stand her."

Disliking someone can mean finding someone unbearable to see or be around. It's a strong aversion to someone. Did you ever play with bar magnets in science class? A magnet has a (+) pole and a (-) pole. Opposite poles will attract and the magnets will gravitate and snap together quickly. But like poles will repel. If you face the (+) pole of one magnet bar towards the (+) pole of another magnet bar, the bars will push against each other and repel strongly. They cannot come together unless a strong force pushes them together. That's another image of disliking—being completely repelled by someone, or only getting along when you are forced together. Another definition would be feeling abhorrence for the person. Strong dislike can also be hatred.

We know who the challenging people are. Perhaps a particular woman has betrayed your confidence. Maybe she gossips. She flirts with the man in your life. She competes with you, or she boasts about herself. Perhaps she finds ways to insult you or put you down. Or maybe you struggle with feelings of jealousy or pride toward her. There are many different reasons why we might struggle, but the truth is we do struggle with liking some of our sisters!

PATTERNS OF ANTIPATHY IN THE KINGDOM

Queen Antipathy (or as I prefer—Queen Dislike) is a major problem, and she's very common, even in church. I have heard so many women talk about how they don't "like" someone. It's a huge divider. Let's look at some

The Queen of Antipathy

of the weaknesses in our relational habits as women of God and start to get a picture of how this dislike concept works. We will start with some food for thought—an example from sorority life:

Sororities: Division and Solidarity

I'm not in a sorority, but when I was in college I had the opportunity to experience and observe some aspects of sorority life. Now, I don't know how every sorority works, but the sororities I was around had this concept called "hood." Hood, put plainly, was about having your sister's back. It was showing solidarity at all times. It was always looking out for the interests of your sister—never ever just yourself. Having hood meant never making your sister look bad in front of other people, never trying to outshine her and make yourself look better than her, and never letting an outsider do harm to her so much as it was in your power.

The funny thing about the whole concept was there were many people within these Greek organizations who couldn't stand each other. And I'm not just talking about one sorority versus the other (although there was some of that too), but I am talking about women in the same organization. I have seen women in the same sorority downright despise each other. Yet, the concept of hood still remained. The requirement to have hood for your sister was beyond personal squabbles and bad blood. It overrode disliking. You might despise her, but you better show a united front and have her back before other people. That was hood, to the best of my knowledge.

"Hood" in the Kingdom

Now, I don't think the people of God should take their cues about how to live from the world. It just doesn't make sense. In a perfect world, the people of God would be the example for the world to follow, not the other way around. But unfortunately, this is not a perfect world, and the people of God have weak spots, and thus there are certain ways in which we could at least learn a few things from what we see in the world. It's unfortunate, but true. From my experience with sororities, I would not suggest the women of God pattern themselves after sororities in every way. I do, however, think we could use a little bit of that hood concept. At least sororities know how to band together when they need to. Have you ever seen it, maybe at a party or on campus? If one of the girls runs into a problem, suddenly you've got twenty others right there backing her up. At that point, division ceases.

Coming up Short

I fail to see that kind of solidarity between the women of God. In fact, I first noticed it when God brought it to my attention regarding my own feelings toward a certain woman. I knew she was a Christian, but I just didn't like her. I didn't like her personality, I didn't like her behavior, I didn't like her way of doing and saying things, and I preferred to just keep away. But God said to me—you may not like this person, but even the sororities have hood—you don't even have that and this is your sister in Christ! Ouch! I was pretty blown away by that. Again, I didn't feel God was suggesting I become like the sorority women. But He did point out a major weakness in the Kingdom, particularly between women. We also should have that kind of fierce dedication to one another, and an unconditional commitment to looking out for our sisters' best interests. It's kind of like the story of the female chimpanzees from chapter two. And we especially need to learn how to show a united front! Sororities understand that showing division makes the whole organization look bad. Well, in the kingdom of God, our unity is especially critical, both for our healthy functioning and for our ability to be a witness in the world. In John 17:23, Jesus prays, "May they be brought to complete unity to let the world know that you sent me and have loved them even as you have loved me." Part of being a "light" in the world is showing unity. Unfortunately, Queen Dislike kind of messes that up for us women sometimes!

The Queen of Antipathy

Getting Caught Up

What the Lord showed me back when I stubbornly disliked a few particular women was this: sometimes we just get far too caught up in disliking people—particularly other women. The kingdom of God is not really about that—the kingdom of God is bigger than that. To a certain degree, the kingdom of God is about some form of "hood." It's about being unified and seeking the common good. It's about putting others before ourselves, serving others, and protecting others. It's about loyalty! That does not mean we are going to be crazy about everyone's personality traits, everyone's qualities, and everyone's habits, because we certainly will not. That's guaranteed. But, the problem is many of us get caught up at the disliking phase. We fail to move on and fail to continually show loyalty, solidarity, support, and commitment despite our personal issues. That's the element of sorority life that I realized I was missing in some of my relationships. Some sorority girls can set aside their differences long enough to settle a problem and show unity, but I was getting so caught up in disliking certain women that I didn't set it aside and continue to show the type of loyalty and sisterhood that I should have. You're not going to "like" everybody (prefer to be around them and thoroughly enjoy their company), but there is a problem when the main thing you think about someone is, "I don't like her!" That sort of thinking is letting petty issues cloud your vision of the larger picture—we are all sisters in Christ.

The Selective Liking Trap!

Now here's another problem. We don't always notice when we have a problem disliking people—why? Because often we are loving, generous, understanding, and kind—to people we like! Disliking women is not about whether or not you are a generally nice person. In fact, you don't get to see whether or not you pass the Queen Antipathy test until you come up against some people you don't particularly like—the challenging individuals.

These people are easy to avoid, and while some degree of distance can certainly be a blessing, avoidance altogether is not the answer. But this test doesn't come until you encounter people you find hard to like. And what's more, you don't get brownie points if you are only kind to the people you like. Let's check out this section of Scripture in Matthew 5, which says, "If you love those who love you, what reward will you get? Are not even the tax collectors doing that? And if you greet only your brothers, what are you doing more than others? Do not even pagans do that? Be perfect, therefore, as your heavenly Father is perfect" (Matthew 5:46–48).

In this passage, Jesus is talking mainly about treatment of enemies, but in verse forty-four, He also mentions "those who persecute you." According to the Lord, we are rewarded when we love our enemies. How much more, then, should we love our mere annoyers, irritators, and instigators, particularly the ones who belong to the body of Christ? The main thing to remember is that you don't get credit when you only have the right heart towards the people you love and get along with. You must have that same heart toward others as well, including those you don't like, to get credit in God's sight.

THE MAIN PROBLEMS WITH QUEEN ANTIPATHY (QUEEN DISLIKE!)

Low Tolerance

Ephesians 4:2 says, "Be completely humble and gentle; be patient, bearing with one another in love." I like the way the New Living Translation puts it: "Always be humble and gentle. Be patient with each other, making allowance for each other's faults because of your love." Other versions, like the King James Version, also use the word "long-suffering" for patience. The point is that part of getting along with others is simply bearing with stuff. It doesn't mean condoning sin or enjoying people's weaknesses. It means bearing it. When I think of the word "bear," I think of carrying

The Queen of Antipathy

something. I can't say to someone, "Here, get on my back! Just leave off your feet, I won't carry your feet." The example is absurd, yes. But that's how relationships are. We have to bear with the entire person; it's all or nothing. I also get the picture of standing with a weight on my back. When more weight is added, bearing it just means not collapsing, but continuing to stand under the pressure without casting it off. In other words, when I encounter the pressure and difficulty of relationships I might not like, I am exhorted to keep standing under it. True unity means bearing with people, which requires patience, or "long-suffering." Bearing with people is not always pleasant; often it requires suffering through the bad in order to get to the good.

I know many, if not all, of my best friendships involved us bearing with one another at one point. All of us agree that God picked us out to be friends—we didn't pick each other. So when God first put us together, there was a lot of abrasion. We definitely didn't see eye to eye on things and at points we just did not like each other. But we were willing to be patient and suffer through the process of coming into one accord, and as we each grew in the Lord and in our understanding of unity, we became very close, dear friends. But it took time, patience, and just putting up with each other sometimes. Had we been impatient and just left during the hard times when all we could see was our dislikes, we would have missed out on some of the best friendships we'd ever have.

Queen Antipathy, on the other hand, does not like to bear with others. As soon as she doesn't like something about someone, she loses tolerance for the person and the relationship. When we let ourselves become this way, we fail to practice bearing with one another. Now, I am not saying we should view relationships merely as thorns in our sides, or engage in deep relationships with unhealthy people. We can't always afford to be close to people who will harm us, and we must look to God for discernment in those situations. But we do need to accept the fact that most relationships will come with dislikes that we need to be patient with and bear under.

Dethroning the Queen

Focusing on our dislikes keeps us from doing that.

Undermining Value

Another danger of dislike is the temptation to undermine the other person's value. If I am constantly rehashing what I do not like about a certain woman, how likely am I to regard her as a child of God? How likely am I to remember that she, too, is "fearfully and wonderfully made?" (Psalms 139:14). I know I have a tendency to forget that pretty quickly. When people get on my nerves, their worth and value is not at the forefront of my mind. When unchecked, losing sight of people's value can lead to sinful attitudes about people. Even God, who knows all of our sins, issues, problems, and hang-ups, never forgets our value. We need to strive to be the same way.

Compromises Our Love

Just in case there's any confusion, love is absolutely vital for followers of Christ. Love is the greatest commandment. If we don't love, then the Bible says we don't know God! 1 John 4:7, 8 says, "Dear friends, let us love one another, for love comes from God. Everyone who loves has been born of God and knows God. Whoever does not love does not know God, because God is love." And not only does not loving people keep us from knowing God, but failing to love people also means we don't truly love God. 1 John 4:20 says, "If anyone says, 'I love God,' yet hates his brother, he is a liar. For anyone who does not love his brother, whom he has seen, cannot love God, whom he has not seen." It is of the utmost importance that we love each other if we are to be true followers of Christ.

Now, where does this fit into liking? Getting too caught up in disliking people can compromise our ability to love them. When you rattle off in your mind the things you do not like about someone, how can you be patient? Kind? How can you keep from being self-seeking, or from not

The Queen of Antipathy

keeping records of wrongs? These are aspects of love that are very difficult when we are focused on disliking people. True, we can love people we don't care for. I am not suggesting we force ourselves into liking other women in order to love them. But I am saying that those women who always cry, "I don't like her!" are in a very poor position to attempt to love. If dislike is all you see, then you will be unable to love.

Enemy Mentality

Once again, like many other Queen Bee problems, antipathy creates the dreaded enemy mentality—we talked about this issue in chapters four and five. Women of God are called to view each other as sisters. We are family, part of one body, and we need each other to function. We are not rivals. Unfortunately, however, one of the main results of the Queen Bee mentality is making women into enemies. Disliking each other certainly promotes that enemy mentality. In fact, when you hear women talking about other women they dislike, they sound like enemies, don't they? Usually women who dislike each other aren't merely teammates working out a disagreement; they generally sound more like full-blown rivals. We must remember that we are on the same team. No petty issue, disagreement, or incompatibility in taste or personality should ever drive us to regard each other as enemies. If two women both love God and pursue His righteousness, there is no reason why one should prematurely label the other one as an enemy, but focusing on our dislikes promotes that kind of animosity.

ANY SUGGESTIONS?

We've established some fundamental problems that can arise from disliking other women: having low tolerance, undermining a woman's value, compromising your ability to love, and developing an enemy mentality. But what on earth can we do about the problem? We can practice the things we mentioned earlier, such as patiently bearing with one another, valuing disliked women, and continuing to practice sisterly love with loyalty. Here are some other steps to prevent and offset the rule of Queen Antipathy in our relationships:

1. Manage your thoughts. In 1 Corinthians 6:12b, Paul says, "I will not be mastered by anything." That even includes our thought process! It is important to exercise control over one's thoughts, particularly when it comes to disliking women. Choose not to fixate on the negative, for that will only lead to greater bitterness, but do as Philippians 4:8 says, "Finally, brothers, whatever is true, whatever is noble, whatever is right, whatever is pure, whatever is lovely, whatever is admirable—if anything is excellent or praiseworthy—think about such things." The key with thoughts is what we dwell on. If your thoughts are locations, where do you live? Where do you spend time? We cannot always stop thoughts from coming to us, but we can always help what we dwell on. We can stop thoughts from brewing. Sometimes our thoughts are like a broken record. I know my mind races, especially about the things that irritate me. Well, sometimes we need to just change the record! Good fruit comes from good trees, so how can peaceful, harmonious relationships exist when we are constantly thinking negative thoughts about a person? Manage your thoughts—choose to fixate on the good and not fixate on the bad.

2. Focus on what you can do: practice harmony. You cannot make yourself like somebody's personality, so don't even try to. God knew we weren't all going to like each other. So, instead of draining yourself trying to make yourself enjoy someone who simply doesn't rub you the right way, instead focus on what you can do. Ephesians 4:3 says, "Make every effort to keep the unity of the Spirit through the bond of peace." We can't change our preferences, but we can always strive for peace and harmony.

The Queen of Antipathy

Instead of fixating on your limits (i.e. ways in which you'll never get along with certain women), think about ways you can create an atmosphere of peace and harmony despite the differences. Strive to show a united front, and commit to loyalty, despite your dislikes.

3. Change your paradigm. A paradigm is a perspective that guides your behavior. Too many women operate out of the paradigm: I don't like her! That paradigm sets a negative tone for all interactions. It creates limits and usually results in bad relationships. Try changing your paradigm to: How can I love her? That paradigm creates opportunities. It offers you the chance to find ways to operate in sisterhood instead of animosity, even if you dislike some things about the woman.

4. Change your labels. Changing your labels comes along with changing your paradigm. Often the women we dislike get permanently categorized into the "dislike" category. It's like taking one of those big rubber stamps and marking her file: "DISLIKED!" Categorizing women this way will only limit our interactions with them. It is a cue to us to put distance between the woman and ourselves or assume an antagonistic relationship. Instead, try stamping those files with the stamp that says, "Sister in Christ." We often forget that women we dislike are still our sisters in the Lord. Instead of labeling a woman with "dislike," label her as a child or God, one to whom you are linked in the body of Christ.

5. Keep the big picture in mind. Sometimes we just need to take a step back and "zoom out" a little bit. The bigger picture is that we are the body of Christ. We have a true commission to be a light in this world. We also have a very real enemy. We need to consider eternity, not just this world. Often, however, we forget these things, or simply put them out of our minds.

Dethroning the Queen

We are more focused on the petty details of our personal squabbles and arguments than on the larger picture. Petty issues can be a big distraction. Traveling demonstrates this concept. My freshman year of college ended with several social concerns. I was all worked up about a guy I had feelings for and was wondering what would happen over the summer. I was worried about whether or not I was going to get involved in sorority life. I was upset about a negative interaction I'd had with someone that I didn't get to patch up before the year ended. These were the thoughts swarming in my head—they seemed so important! Then a couple weeks later, I went to Mexico on a mission trip, and it blew my mind. Perhaps you've had similar experiences. Something about traveling makes you realize how silly and trivial some of your daily concerns can be. I remember thinking that none of the things I was worried about were really that important in the long run, and by the end of the trip, I didn't care about any of that stuff I had been thinking about before. Getting just a slightly larger perspective of the world helped me prioritize my thoughts. Sometimes we need to do the same thing. If we would just stop to think about larger kingdom issues, I think we would get over the roadblock of disliking other women and learn how to prioritize between petty and important issues, and do a better job at living in harmony.

One Last Thought: Addressing "Fakeness"

Now I have heard many women claim that to smile in an enemy's face is to be fake. I truly want to challenge that notion; I believe that thought is completely worldly. No—we are not called to be deceitful, but Jesus never calls for us to mistreat our enemies. Instead, we are commanded to bless them, pray for them, love them, do good to them, lend to them, and even

The Queen of Antipathy

help and serve them (Luke 6:27, 28, Romans 12:20)! People should not be able to distinguish whom you like from whom you don't based on your treatment of them. Again, do not be deceitful or malicious in dealing with enemies, and certainly do not slander them in secret. Do not say things to them you do not mean. But do not succumb to the world's thinking and be deceived into believing that showing kindness to your enemies is a sign of fakeness. In reality, it is a sign of holiness, obedience, meekness, and self-control.

IN CONCLUSION: THE ROLE OF DISCERNMENT

We are not going to become best friends with all the women who work our nerves. It's not realistic, and in some cases, it's not even wise. It is important to use discernment when establishing boundaries in relationships. Continue to choose your councilors, confidants, and close friends carefully. Just remember to treat the other women as sisters as well, for we are all part of one body. Remember the "hood" concept! And remember the importance of love, because love is the key to fellowship with God and one another.

Prayer

Dear Lord,

Thank You for loving me enough to place sisters in my life, even when I don't get along with them all. I acknowledge that all of Your followers, even the ones I find unpleasant, are Your daughters and I should treat them as sisters with great worth. Forgive me for letting dislike dominate my interactions with certain women. Help me to set those petty issues aside and focus on loving all the members of Your kingdom. Give me the grace to be patient, and to bear up under difficult and trying relationships. Give me Your heart toward the people I don't get along with as I continue to use wisdom about my relationships with those women. Help me see the bigger picture and have true kingdom-mindedness. Thank

Dethroning the Queen

You for already sending Your Holy Spirit to help me with this. Create harmony in all my relationships. I ask these things in Jesus' Name. Amen.

Memory Verse

"Anyone who claims to be in the light but hates his brother is still in the darkness."
1 John 2:9

Reflection Questions

Who are some of the women you struggle with liking? Why?

Is it a reflection of you, them, neither, or both? What, if anything, can you take responsibility for?

What are some of the positive aspects of those women?

What ways can you sow harmony in these relationships?

What, if anything, can you gain from being around them?

Would forgiveness help you get along with any of these women? (If so, work on forgiving them!)

The Queen of Antipathy

What are some of the "petty issues" you can "bear" with?

What will suffer if you fixate on your dislikes?

In what areas can you benefit from a bigger perspective?

Action Plan!

Identify a woman you struggle with liking. Make a point not to dwell on her bad side. Instead, think about the big picture and how you are linked in the kingdom of God. Try to consider her good points (no matter how obscure they may seem!) and let that positive meditation affect your dealings with her.

CHAPTER SEVEN

The Queen of Discord

"Leave your gift there in front of the altar.
First go and be reconciled to your brother; then come and offer your gift."
MATTHEW 5:24

QUEEN DISCORD REIGNS when women are in disagreement. She exists in a perpetual state of conflict. Essentially, discord is what happens when two or more people are not reconciled. For instance, have you ever seen two family members get into an argument that separates them for an extended period of time? All of a sudden they no longer speak, and even if they must come together in the same room for family gatherings, there is no fellowship or peace between them. That's discord. It is not just disagreeing; it is an ongoing state of disagreement. Queen Discord is about severed and interrupted relationships, not merely differences of opinion.

Women experience discord for many reasons. A disagreement happens and is never resolved. One person gets offended and the issue is never addressed. Two women fail to come to a mutual understanding. One person fails to see something from the other person's perspective. Miscommunication, misinterpretation, assumptions, hurtful words, and unspoken words—all of these things can play a part in discord. Some women are in conflict simply because they did not address an offense in a productive way. It's like Proverbs 18:19 says, "An offended brother is more unyielding than a fortified city, and disputes are like the barred gates of a citadel." Someone gets offended, and she is no longer interested in anything the other person has to say.

Others of us are used to being in conflict. We consider it normal, and take it as merely a fact of life. Perhaps it's something you take for granted or have always experienced. Maybe you've never been taught differently. You think there are those women you like and get along with, and those you can't stand and will have nothing to do with. Well, let me tell you: discord is not healthy! It is not good to walk around in a perpetual state of conflict with someone. Even if there are no more fights or arguments, the separation and disjointedness that discord creates is unhealthy. This is especially true for women who follow God.

EXPLAINING RECONCILIATION

Reconciliation is the opposite of discord. Whereas discord involves separation, reconciliation involves bringing back together. Reconciliation is a very important concept, so let's look at the definition. *The New International Webster's Concise Dictionary* defines the word reconcile this way:

1. "To bring back to friendship after estrangement."
2. "To settle or adjust, as a quarrel."
3. "To bring to acquiescence, content, or submission."
4. "To make or show to be consistent or congruous; harmonize."[1]

Reconciliation is about creating agreement, settling differences, re-establishing disjointed relationships, and creating (or recreating) harmony between people.

PROBLEMS WITH DISCORD

There are many practical and spiritual reasons why discord is problematic. Let's discuss a few.

The Queen of Discord

Discord Brings Judgment

Consider this passage from Matthew 5.

You have heard that it was said to the people long ago, "Do not murder, and anyone who murders will be subject to judgment." But I tell you that anyone who is angry with his brother will be subject to judgment. Again, anyone who says to his brother, "Raca," is answerable to the Sanhedrin. But anyone who says, "You fool!" will be in danger of the fire of hell.

Therefore, if you are offering your gift at the altar and there remember that your brother has something against you, leave your gift there in front of the altar. First go and be reconciled to your brother; then come and offer your gift (Matthew 5:21–24).

How many times do women gather together in church to offer praise and worship to God when they have failed to be reconciled to each other? There is a time for "anger." In fact, we see God's anger, both as the Father and as the Son. You may be familiar with the story of when Jesus got angry with moneychangers in the temple, or when he became angry with the Pharisees. But I believe one of the problems, as demonstrated by Jesus' command in the second part of the Scripture, is remaining at odds with a sister in Christ. If you're in church and remember that someone has something against you, or vice versa, the Bible commands us to go and be reconciled. But remaining in a state of discord brings judgment.

Discord is Cancerous to the Body of Christ

We've talked in chapter two about how dangerous division in the body of Christ is. After all, if the people of God are likened to a physical body, then division between the members is comparable to cancer! Discord is the opposite of unity and harmonious functioning. It results in disjointed members who are often unable to work together properly. In other words, discord is detrimental to the functioning of God's church.

Dethroning the Queen

Discord Gives the Devil a Foothold

Ephesians 4:26, 27 says, "'In your anger do not sin': Do not let the sun go down while you are still angry, and do not give the devil a foothold." I can certainly testify about that. There have been times when I was offended or upset with someone, and if I tried to go to bed without addressing the problem, I would feel like the offense would just blow up inside of me! When you are not quick to be reconciled, the enemy can use that delay time, and before you know it, you are angrier with the person than you were initially. Unaddressed problems can take root and grow. Rehashing offenses can make them seem bigger and can escalate the emotions. It's almost like a split end that needs to be trimmed before the strand continues to split. The enemy likes to work at untrimmed split ends in our relationships. That's why it is important to resolve problems before there is discord.

Discord Does Not Lead to Righteousness

Anger is at the root of many conflicts. It has the same separating effect as discord. James 1:20 says, "Man's anger does not bring about the righteous life that God desires." When we remain upset with one another, we run the risk of letting sin get into our lives. It is like a bad seed that can also grow to bear fruit. The fruit of righteousness does not come from the seed of discord. If we want to be followers of Christ, we should do everything we can to lead upright lives, including staying away from discord, which dims our light.

CAUSES OF DISCORD

Even though there can be a million different issues people can disagree about or become offended by, there are some general concepts about how discord and conflict can happen. Let's look at some of the ways:

The Queen of Discord

Handling Problems Poorly—Or Making Them Worse

Sometimes we reinforce disunity with the way we handle the original source of the problem. We reinforce problems with distance, mean comments, slander and back-talk, gossip, bias, miscommunication, dwelling on our own assumptions, and other things. I have been in arguments that began over very minor issues that could have been overlooked. But when handled poorly, for instance, talking about the person or refusing to drop an "attitude," blows the problem out of proportion, and suddenly the two of us aren't even speaking. When we mishandle disagreements, we can enter into discord.

Manipulation and Strategic Relationships

We all know that women have a way of attacking each other without laying a hand on each other. Often, this is done by attacking other women by using relationships strategically. When one woman is offended, she desires to rally support for her cause. It may be malicious, or it may just be an unwise way of seeking affirmation. In any case, it's wrong. When the offended woman (who is probably biased) begins telling other women about the offense, women who were initially uninvolved suddenly turn to comfort the offended woman. By the time the offender comes around, everyone hates her and is already on the other woman's side.

Let me tell you from experience; manipulation and strategic use of relationships only causes mass discord. It does nothing to solve the problem; it only makes it bigger by getting other people involved. It's a lose-lose situation: less resolution, bigger problem. As women, we were made to be relational creatures. When we are wounded, we go to our relationships. Many times we are not comfortable when our best friend is on good terms with someone we're in conflict with—we want her to take our side until the issue is resolved (if it ever is). This behavior, however, does not promote the love and unity that should characterize the body of Christ. What a terrible feeling to be the poor woman against whom the whole community of women has turned! (I have been on both sides of the equation.) When we give in to the temptation to rally the support of others and attack others with relationships, whether intentionally or not, we create mass discord.

Harping on Every Problem

Proverbs 19:11 says, "A man's wisdom gives him patience; it is to his glory to overlook an offense." Sometimes we just need to get over it. You don't always have to call a board meeting because somebody stepped on your toe in the hallway. Not every minor irritation is worth a livid email or an impromptu powwow. Proverbs advises us to just relax a little bit and be patient. There is definitely a time to speak up (as we will discuss in the next point), but there is also a time to simply let things go. In other words, pick your battles. Be patient enough with people to let them grow out of their offenses, instead of nagging them out of their offenses. Try to give people enough grace to overlook the little stuff. It will operate to your benefit as well as theirs.

Keeping It Inside

My personality is not naturally confrontational. (That's part of why it's so tempting to just use friendships strategically—it's easier to just talk to other people than to confront the offender!) I may be angry as all get-out on the inside, but I used to really struggle when I actually had to come forward with an offense, especially to a friend. I didn't (and still don't) like making other people uncomfortable. That's partially because I am sensitive and can be somewhat easily offended. I knew how it felt for my feelings to be hurt, so I was reluctant to make others feel that way. As a result, I kept a lot of issues to myself instead of speaking up to the person involved.

Anyway, silence turned out to be a very bad way to go. I ended up being an example of what happens when Proverbs 19:11 (overlooking offenses) is practiced incorrectly. I would outwardly brush off offenses and

The Queen of Discord

think to myself, "I don't want to make a big deal about it," "I shouldn't say anything," "Well, maybe if it comes up again," "Well, this is different," or, "I don't want to cause problems." I would find ways to try and brush off the problem or delay confrontation, but the truth was, inwardly I was still holding on to those negative emotions. Keeping things inside led to resentment, and resentment can be a major precursor to discord.

Furthermore, my resentment from keeping things in biased my perspective of the person. My emotions created a self-fulfilling prophecy. A self-fulfilling prophecy is an expectation that you inadvertently force to come true. For example, I would get offended, I didn't say anything, I held on to the negative emotions, I fell into resentment, resentment made me see the person in a negative light, and because I was always expecting to see the negative in her, that's what I saw. Often when you expect women to be offensive, you find reasons to be offended that you might not have noticed otherwise. You translate ambiguous actions as being negative. In addition, negative expectations alter your treatment of someone, which can cause them to treat you differently in turn.

Essentially, keeping issues bottled in can do a lot of damage. It can breed resentment, which will only increase discord. It also minimizes (and often completely eradicates) opportunities for reconciliation. It leaves the door wide open for miscommunication and misunderstanding. It does not provide the other person a chance to redeem herself or to even become aware of her actions. While it is noble to overlook an offense, you should only attempt to do so if you can truly overlook it. But do not try to overlook a problem when you know you are simply going to end up keeping the issue bottled in. Those feelings can create negative expectations about the person that bias your interpretation of and experience with that person.

Misplaced Aggression

Remember what we talked about in the chapter about jealousy? We discussed James chapter four, where James says we fight and quarrel because we don't have what we want (James 4:1, 2). If one woman is lonely for romance, it's not a mystery that she should end up in conflict with the new woman who instantly got attention from one of the attractive men in the group! Honestly, sometimes the only reason women fight is because we are upset about something we don't have, and we take it out on other women instead of getting on our knees in prayer and presenting our hearts to God. We fail to get real with God: "God, I don't feel pretty!" "God, I don't feel loved!" "God, I don't feel good enough!" "God, I don't feel accepted!" "God, I don't feel valuable!" Instead, we direct our feelings and hurts on other women, getting upset with them when really it has nothing to do with them and everything to do with us.

Lack of Love

One day during my devotional time with God, I was reading the story of the Tower of Babel, and the Holy Spirit revealed something to me that helped me understand a conflict I was having at the time, and it may shed light here. In Genesis chapter eleven, back in the early days after the flood, it says, "The whole world had one language and a common speech" (Genesis 11:1). At some point, the people proudly decided to build a tower so they could reach the heavens, but to prevent humans from being able to rally together and execute all their bad ideas, the Bible says, "The Lord confused the language of the whole world" (Genesis 11:9). Now, many people take this story as an explanation of the origin of the various languages spoken on earth. But in my devotional time, I thought to myself—not only did men begin to speak different languages that day, but they also lost a certain ability to come together in one accord that day. It's as if our ability to understand each other decreased, even within the same language. Our ability to effectively communicate was confused. Haven't you seen people try to work out an argument, and no matter what they say, they simply fail to understand each other? I personally believe it goes back to this story of the Tower of Babel—the day

The Queen of Discord

when our language and communication was confused by God. Now this does not mean harmony and understanding are impossible. Look at the next piece. The Lord then took me to 1 Corinthians 13:1. It says, "If I speak in the tongues [or other languages] of men and of angels, but have not love, I am only a resounding gong or a clanging cymbal." Picture someone's speech being like a "resounding gong" or a "clanging cymbal." It would sound like annoying chaos, or mass confusion. So, in other words, even if you were able to speak every single language on earth fluently, and you were even able to speak every language in heaven, without love, you're always going to sound like chaotic noise, no matter what you say! It's as if love even smoothes out communication. Without love, we'd be forever subject to the confusion-prone communication from the Tower of Babel. Sometimes, words simply won't do it, and the only thing that breaks through is love. I have had times where a sister and I would try to talk things through—and that does work sometimes—but other times it's like we just talk until we're blue in the face. But seeing how she comes to my side to pray for me when I'm going through personal trauma, or getting a nice card in the middle of the day for no reason, or even just getting a hug when we can't explain ourselves any more—sometimes that's the only thing that can pierce through the discord: acts of love. I believe much discord can be attributed to too much talk and not enough expression of love. After all, even when we are mad at somebody, we often don't hate him or her. Sometimes all the other person needs is to see that your heart toward her is still love.

ADDRESSING THESE PROBLEMS

Due to the many issues that can arise when problems go unaddressed, here are some basic guidelines to settle conflict and avoid discord.

1. Settle issues quickly. Matthew 5:25a says, "Settle matters quickly with your adversary who is taking you to court." In other words,

get to the matter quickly, before you get to the judge! And we've already talked about Ephesians 4:26, 27, which says, "Do not let the sun go down while you are still angry and do not give the devil a foothold." Settling issues quickly helps keep them from growing into bigger problems, warranting bigger punishments, and creating bigger divides.

2. Use others as arbiters, not strategic ammunition. In the Bible, a relationship is not a weapon, but rather a tool used to bring peace. Matthew 18:15, 16 says, "If your brother sins against you, go and show him his fault, just between the two of you. If he listens to you, you have won your brother over. But if he will not listen, take one or two others along, so that 'every matter may be established by the testimony of two or three witnesses'." Notice, the first step is trying to settle the matter in private. I don't understand people who always want to announce their issues with others in front of crowds, or even groups of friends. It's particularly confusing when it happens amongst Christians. I believe the order in this passage of Matthew is much more respectful and discreet. If you have a problem with Ericka, talk to Ericka. There is no need to talk to Ericka in front of an entire group. That only promotes shame and distrust, not openness and honesty. Now if Ericka refuses to listen, then you can bring along Sandra and Debbie. But first try talking to Ericka alone. And certainly do not talk to Sandra and Debbie before you talk to Ericka. People are only to be used as agents of arbitration when needed.

3. Speak up. The Bible exhorts us to, "[Speak] the truth in love" (Ephesians 4:15a). Be gentle and loving in your speech, but do not sit and brood on your grievances in silence. Get them up to the surface so you can be reconciled quickly.

4. Go to God with your desires. Often we fight because we don't

have what we want. Don't take it out on your sisters in a fight. Let it out to God on your knees in prayer.

5. Speak the language of love. When you are failing to get your point across with words, just show the person that you love them. Speak a kind word. Give her a hug. Pray for her (and not that she would be delivered, but that she would be blessed). Love can pierce through walls that words cannot.

6. Let God fight your battles. It is much easier to be reconciled when you realize you are not in charge of justice (we will discuss judgment in the next chapter). You do not have to hold out until the other person comes clean before you have peace toward her. Be reconciled and let God handle the justice. Look at David in 1 Samuel 24! David was severely wronged and mistreated by Saul, yet David honored Saul—the very man who was trying to kill him! After all, 2 Chronicles 20:15b says, "The battle is not yours, but God's." Sometimes if we would only lay hold of this concept, we would release some of the battles that we try to fight.

7. Lay down boundaries. Boundaries are extremely important in relationships. If you create appropriate boundaries, you can release some wrongs with the knowledge that you have done your part in preventing a re-occurrence of the same problems. For example, you cannot control the fact that your friend Tina can be flakey. You can't control any of her weaknesses or character flaws. But you can, for instance, choose to stop relying on her for a ride somewhere. Plan to ride with Rachel and then you will not spend all day upset with Tina for canceling or arriving late. Boundaries can often help prevent future discord.

8. Finally, forgive. This is something many of us are simply unwilling to do. Forgiveness is a humongous part of reconciliation. Always show others an abundance of forgiveness. In Matthew

18:22, Jesus says to forgive someone, "Not seven times, but seventy-seven times." Why? Because God has shown us an abundance of forgiveness. It was His merciful sacrifice of His Son that made a way for us to be reconciled to Him, so we must also show the same mercy toward each other for us to be reconciled to each other. Just remember—you will never be required to forgive others more than God has forgiven you. Matthew 6:14, 15 says, "For if you forgive men when they sin against you, your heavenly Father will also forgive you. But if you do not forgive men their sins, your Father will not forgive your sins."

Concluding

Always remember that discord is not in God's design. It is His will that we live in perfect unity and harmony with one another. It is not healthy to let disagreements fester, or to fail to resolve problems. Instead, focus on reconciliation. Unfortunately, there are no step-by-step instructions for solving each relational problem, because the issues vary so widely, but if you maintain a general tendency toward reconciliation, you will be in a much better position. Also, always keep an abundance of forgiveness.

The Queen of Discord cannot reign if there is to be a healthy body of women within the body of Christ. Instead of coming together on Sunday mornings with hidden conflict with other women beneath the surface, ask the Holy Spirit to help you maintain harmony with other sisters in the body of Christ and re-establish harmony with others!

Prayer

Dear Heavenly Father,
Thank You for being the God of peace. It is Your will that we should dwell together in unity with other members of the body. You do not desire conflict and discord, but rather harmony and reconciliation. Lord, please forgive me for letting offenses fester and mishandling problems when they

The Queen of Discord

arose. Forgive me for letting long-term conflict exist between my sister and me. Now I invite You to help this situation to change. Right now, I may not see how to resolve the issue, but You, God of all peace, know how we can dwell together in unity. So I invite You now. Thank You for your heart of redemption. Give me a greater heart of forgiveness and mercy. I ask this in Jesus' Name. Amen.

Memory Verse

"First go and be reconciled to your brother; then come and offer your gift."
MATTHEW 5:24b

Reflection Questions

Can you think of anyone with whom you are not currently reconciled? How long has there been discord?

What originally caused the problem?

Is there anything that could have been done to handle the problem better?

Has the issue grown? What are the problems now?

Is there room for forgiveness or overlooking offenses? If so, are you ready to do that?

Is there room for asking forgiveness or pardon? If so, are you ready to ask for it?

Are there any boundaries or other changes that you can make to prevent the problem from re-occurring in the future?

Action Plan!

If you have anyone to forgive, speak to the person and communicate your forgiveness if the person is receptive. Ask the Holy Spirit how to go about doing this. Also, express any overdue apologies and ask for forgiveness. Finally, find a way to show the person you're in conflict with an act of love.

CHAPTER EIGHT

The Queen of Judgment

"Do not judge, or you too will be judged."

MATTHEW 7:1

WHAT ONE ISSUE seems to be the cause of so many people's reservations about going to church? What turns people off of Christianity? What scares people about attending a Christian fellowship or service, and makes people feel intimidated and defensive? One of the big issues is judgment. Christians tend to have a bad rap for being judgmental. I do not believe that is totally the fault of believers. It is often the case that people who feel convicted prefer to label others as judgmental instead of receiving correction. Nevertheless, there is some judgment going on in the Kingdom, and we need to take responsibility for that. Have you ever been judged by a woman in church? Have you ever judged a woman in church? The likely answer to at least one of those questions is yes. We are going to talk about Queen Judgment in this chapter and attempt to break her influence in our relationships.

DEFINING JUDGMENT

The word *judge* can be used in two ways: one as a noun when referring to a person, i.e. in a courtroom, and two as a verb when referring to the action of judging someone. Both definitions shed light on the concept of judgment. *The New International Webster's Concise Dictionary* defines the noun *judge* this way:

1. "An official, elected or appointed, invested with authority to administer legal justice."
2. "In contests, controversies, etc., one who selects the winner, evaluates the merits of contestants, etc."
3. "One qualified to have opinions on the worth or value of something."

The verb form of the word judge is defined this way:

1. "To hear and decide in an official capacity the merits of (a case) or the guilt of (a person)."
2. "To appraise or evaluate."
3. "To act as a judge; sit in judgment."[1]

These definitions are very important if we are to understand judgment. We will come back to them later in this chapter.

JUDGMENT BETWEEN WOMEN: HOW AND WHY WE DO IT

Pride

There are many reasons why women judge each other. For instance, women sometimes judge each other out of pride. We will talk more about pride in chapter twelve. But sometimes we just want to be the Queen Bees sitting on top of the world. Whether we want attention or recognition, beauty or popularity, love, smarts, talent, or praise, we often desire to be the best at something. Judging others is a way to make oneself feel superior to others. It can be a spoken judgment or a thought kept hidden in one's heart. Judging someone is a way of highlighting somebody else's flaws, and some women sinfully judge others when they want to feel better about themselves. I can admit I've done that before! It's not even always conscious, but sometimes thinking of someone else's shortcomings feels comforting and even self-glorifying.

Seeking Validation

Another reason for judging is seeking validation after being offended. Say Natasha flirts with Tina's boyfriend. Tina would be upset and for good reason! But if Tina starts scrutinizing everything about Natasha and making judgments about her clothes, her speech, her character, and her motives, Tina has now moved into a sinful attitude. Sometimes we comfort ourselves with judgments about our enemies. It is a way of seeking validation for our offense. We feel disempowered by being offended, and now we look to judgment for personal empowerment (instead of looking to God!). Though judgment may be driven by pain rather than by cruelty, it is still wrong to take judgment into our own hands—even if the other person has obviously sinned against us!

Jealousy

Sometimes women judge other women out of jealousy. This is a big problem, so we'll spend a little more time talking about it. I can recount times when I was the object of such judgment and perhaps you can too. Here is a story that illustrates how jealousy can lead to judgment. I've always been known as a "girly-girl" so to speak. What people meant by that was I preferred heels to sneakers, and wore skirts voluntarily when others wore jeans. Dressing that way made me feel pretty and feminine. But I distinctly remember being a young teenager and experiencing judgment from other women. A group of us were out at dinner. I was wearing a light purple shirt with a knee-length skirt and some wedge sandals. Pretty, yet modest. Most of the others, on the other hand, had elected to wear pants, khakis, and t-shirts, but I didn't mind being in a skirt—after all, we were at a restaurant. Somehow the conversation at the table shifted to me, and specifically my attire. Some of the girls were commenting that I was always so "dressy," and their tone indicated disapproval. I didn't understand what the huge deal was, but some of the girls continued, suggesting I dress more casually. They even seemed annoyed by my dressing up. (Perturbed preoccupation always reeks of jealousy!) But I was young, and I started to feel bad. I had more sense than to wish I had worn something else, but I was extremely confused at all the preoccupation about me wearing heels and a skirt to a restaurant. After all, my skirt wasn't short; it fell just below my knees! I tried to recover, and asked what the problem was, considering that my skirt was a very modest length and that indecent exposure certainly couldn't be the reason for all the hoopla. Of course, they could not counter that argument, so instead they shifted attention to my shoes. One of the older women remarked that heels are designed to show off the legs, and that toes can be very appealing to a young man. That really did it. Of all the confusing statements anyone could ever make, suggesting that my toes were "appealing" was absolutely insane. I've never had pretty toes! Plus, I actually have huge feet. Polish makes my toes look just decent enough to display in a toe-out sandal, but if I were trying to seduce anyone, I would certainly elect a closed-toe alternative! The older women at the table were being ridiculous. They were not going to let up until I felt bad about myself for some reason. And you know what—I was only fifteen or so, and it worked. I excused myself from the table, went to the restroom, and cried! I felt so judged—publicly and intentionally judged! I felt accused for being a show-off at best, and a beacon of lust at worst! And all I wanted to do was be presentable and pretty. There weren't even any guys present that I was trying to impress. I just wanted to wear my favorite purple shirt and look nice.

That day was a great example of female jealousy-driven judgment at its best (or worst)! Some women judge others because they feel threatened or jealous of another woman, so in response they want to make her feel

The Queen of Judgment

bad so they don't have to. We can't know exactly what's going on in the hearts or minds of women who judge us, but there do seem to be some general trends, and jealousy is one. Instead of accepting that another woman looks pretty, some women want to judge the pretty woman and make her out to be "loose" or "fast" or "fresh," because if they can convince themselves that she is sinful in some way, they don't have to feel bad about themselves. It's harsh and petty, but true! Judgment is often a way women attempt to direct negative feelings about themselves to others. Can you see why dethroning the Queen of Judgment is so necessary?

I have a friend who happens to be light-skinned and have long hair, and recently she felt judged by an entire roomful of black women. Now, for my African-American sisters, you know what that stereotype is like. Historically, lighter-skinned, longer-haired black women have been purported to be superior to darker-skinned, shorter-haired black women. Most of us should know that mentality is just as outdated as racism. Nevertheless, it still haunts many of our interactions. In fact, I've even been guilty of it—assuming that a lighter-skinned woman would be conceited! How terrible! Sadly though, many of us have heard skin color jokes, directed both at light and dark-skinned people. But no matter what actual experiences we may have, prejudice is never acceptable. If anyone should know that, it's us. If you are a brown-skinned woman who was teased by a light-skinned girl on the playground, don't assume every light-skinned woman will turn her nose up at you! Light-skinned women, if you have ever been excluded or rejected by a group of darker-skinned girls on the playground, don't walk around with that chip still on your shoulder when you interact with other dark-skinned black women. We all have to let go of the old baggage and prejudices. That said, my light-skinned, longhaired friend walked into a room at a get-together. I had a great time, but in the car during the ride home, my friend confessed she'd had a miserable time. I had no idea why, since we'd all been hanging together pretty much the entire time. When I asked her, she said it was the icy stares she received from the other women in the room. She said many of the ladies stared at her with looks of disgust or disapproval. That's why, she confessed, she kept finding things to do to help the hostess—just to get a break from the social tension. Many of the black women in the room did not look like my friend, who is tall and naturally attracts attention. My friend confessed that she sometimes experiences automatic judgment from black women who don't look like her, and is treated as if she's some sort of stuck-up snob as soon as she walks in a room!

It's another case of judgment driven by insecurity—women projecting their hang-ups onto other women and trying to impose guilt on them to ward off those they feel threatened by.

Righteousness Gone Wrong

Another reason for judging might even be rooted in a genuine desire for righteousness. Sometimes when we are familiar with biblical standards of living, we don't like to see people violate them. I am naturally an extremely rules-oriented person. I like to follow rules, and I like to see others do the same, but we must remember that God is loving and merciful. Judgment, on the other hand, is arrogant. It becomes more obvious that judgment is arrogant when we find ourselves being the sinners instead of the judges. All of us have sinned, even the devout churchgoers! Righteous anger is not an excuse for judgment. There are endless reasons why women might judge each other, so these are just a few common reasons. In any case, no matter what the reason for judgment, it's always a problem! Let's look at some of the ways judgment creates trouble in our lives.

THE PROBLEMS WITH JUDGING—UNABLE TO JUDGE

Judgment is a big problem, both morally and practically. One of the basic reasons why we shouldn't judge others is because as people, we lack the ability to judge. Here's why:

The Queen of Judgment

Lack of Authority

Unless you have a Juris Doctor degree and are employed in the legal system, you are literally unable to judge anyone. In fact, even if you are a court judge, you are not able to judge people's hearts. People are not qualified to be spiritual or moral judges. Let's again look at the dictionary definition of a judge. We may in certain cases know right from wrong. We may be able to make observations about a situation. But, based on the definition, a judge is an appointed official. That implies authority. God has not given us the authority to judge others. James 4:12 says, "There is only one Lawgiver and Judge, the one who is able to save and destroy. But you—who are you to judge your neighbor?" God is the only one with the authority to judge our hearts, and it's always a bad idea to take something into your own hands that really belongs to God!

Lack of Information

Furthermore, in order to judge, you must first be presented with the full set of facts pertaining to the case. That's why part of the definition of *judge* is to "appraise." An appraisal is an evaluation of the condition of something. It often involves numbers—estimating the worth, cost, or amount of the thing being appraised. Have you ever had an appraisal done on your house? People call appraisers when they want to know how much their house is worth. The appraiser then has to come in and take detailed notes of the entire house, noting everything from the square footage of the house and the number of its rooms down to the condition of the walls, fixtures, ceilings, and floors. Appraising is part of judging. One must gather as many facts as possible in order to analyze and then make a ruling.

We are unable to judge others because we are not omniscient; God is. Can you make a detailed list of everything a person has ever thought, done, or said, as well as itemize all the motives of her heart? Some people arrogantly think they can sum a person up, but it isn't true. We can't even fully know ourselves that way! That's why David prays, "How can I know all the sins lurking in my heart? Cleanse me from these hidden faults" (Psalms 19:12, NLT). Our knowledge is limited, and if we don't even fully know our own hearts, imagine how little we can fully know about someone else's heart! I am not saying we don't know anything, but we certainly don't know nearly enough to judge. Limited knowledge prevents us from being able to judge other people.

When the Bible says God is omniscient, it means He is all knowing. Hebrews 4:13 says, "Nothing in all creation is hidden from God's sight. Everything is uncovered and laid bare before the eyes of him to whom we must give an account." God sees everything. People, on the other hand, only know in part. In 1 Corinthians 13:12b, Paul says, "Now I know in part; then I shall know fully, even as I am fully known." He is mainly emphasizing the fact that our knowledge on this side of heaven is only partial. For that reason, we are unable to judge others.

There is a line in *The Lord of the Rings: The Fellowship of the Ring*[2] (my favorite movie) that is very insightful about judgment. The main character, Frodo, is upset that Gollum—a morally contradictory character whom he finds threatening—is following him. In a moment of anger, Frodo comments, "It's a pity Bilbo didn't kill [Gollum] when he had the chance." But Gandalf, the good wizard, chastises Frodo, saying, "Pity? It was pity that stayed Bilbo's hand. Many that live deserve death. Some that die deserve life. Can you give it to them Frodo? Do not be too eager to deal out death in judgment. Even the very wise cannot see all ends. My heart tells me that Gollum has some part to play yet, for good or ill before this is over. The pity of Bilbo may rule the fate of many." In this quote, Gandalf summarizes much of the problem of judgment. Frodo's lack of both mercy and understanding limits his ability to judge wisely, and ultimately, Frodo is not the one who can deal out reward and punishment. The awesome thing about this part of the movie is the ironic fact that Gandalf's wisdom proves correct. Though in the film Gollum is certainly influenced by evil, he plays a crucial role in the ultimate defeat of the evil Sauron. The same goes for us.

The Queen of Judgment

We cannot see all ends. We cannot see what the dispensing or withholding of mercy affects. We are limited in our understanding of justice, and unfit to judge others.

Marred Creatures

We are also sinful creatures, which hinders our ability to judge. Deuteronomy 32:4 says, "All [God's] ways are just. A faithful God who does no wrong, upright and just is he." Because God is completely just and upright, He is qualified to judge us. Man, on the other hand, is sinful. Matthew 7:4, 5 makes it clear that our own faults get in the way of us being able to accurately see or judge the faults of others. Jesus says only if sin is removed from us can we "see clearly to remove the speck from [our] brother's eye." In Job 34:17a, Elihu exclaims, "Can he who hates justice govern?" In other words, because we, unlike God, are not fully righteous and just, we are unqualified to serve as judges of others in this world.

In addition, as imperfect creatures, we do not perfectly understand justice. That's why mankind is constantly questioning God throughout Scripture and even today. Job questions God, complaining about His treatment of the righteous and the wicked. The Israelites question God in the desert, claiming they were led out of Egypt only to die in the desert. Man questions God because we don't fully understand God or His justice. That's why God reminds us in Isaiah 55:8, 9, "My thoughts are not your thoughts, neither are your ways my ways... As the heavens are higher than the earth, so are my ways higher than your ways and my thoughts than your thoughts." We are unable to judge because our imperfection prohibits us from even fully understanding justice.

Reward and Punishment

In Matthew 10:28, God refers to himself, through Jesus, as "The One who can destroy both soul and body in hell." God is the only one who can ultimately deal out eternal reward and punishment. That is another reason He is the only fit judge. One of the definitions of a judge is one who selects the winner of a contest or competition. Even the judge in a courtroom is able to deal out a sentence. A judge is someone who is able to reward and punish. From an eternal standpoint, we are not able to ultimately punish or reward anyone, we cannot place anyone in heaven or hell, so we are once again found to be unqualified as judges.

Commanded Not to Judge

Not only are we unable to judge, but the Bible is clear that we are commanded by God not to judge others for our own good. Here are some reasons why:

Judging Others Takes our Eyes off of Ourselves

Jesus says in Matthew 7:3–5, "Why do you look at the speck of sawdust in your brother's eye and pay no attention to the plank in your own eye? How can you say to your brother, 'Let me take the speck out of your eye,' when all the time there is a plank in your own eye? You hypocrite, first take the plank out of your own eye, and then you will see clearly to remove the speck from your brother's eye." One of the points Jesus is trying to get across here is that we have our own issues to deal with, and frequently, our issues are bigger than whatever fault we are trying to pick at in someone else. Judging others takes our eyes off of ourselves. We are not commanded to refrain from judging because other people are perfect. We are commanded to refrain from judging because we have plenty of work cut out for us just in dealing with ourselves. After all, 1 Corinthians 11:31 says, "If we judged ourselves, we would not come under judgment." In other words, if we spent time searching our hearts, pinpointing our own sins, and repenting, we would be able to avoid having to be judged by the Lord (at least for those sins). So, one of the reasons we are commanded not to judge others is because we need to focus on the task of searching our own hearts.

The Queen of Judgment

Judging Others Brings Judgment and Condemnation Upon Ourselves

Matthew 7:1 says, "Do not judge, or you too will be judged." That verse is pretty self-explanatory. When we judge others we are really just bringing judgment on ourselves. Paul says it even more clearly: "You, therefore, have no excuse, you who pass judgment on someone else, for at whatever point you judge the other, you are condemning yourself, because you who pass judgment do the same things" (Romans 2:1). Judging someone else is hypocritical, because we are all sinners. The Bible says, "All have sinned and fall short of the glory of God" (Romans 3:23). All of us have done things deserving judgment, so when we judge someone else, our judgment is stored up against ourselves. Judging others is a self-condemning activity!

HOW JUDGMENT HINDERS RELATIONSHIPS

It is pretty obvious that judgment is sort of a downer when it comes to relationships. One problem is that judgment creates distrust. In any relationship, you want to have confidence in someone's integrity regarding you. After all, 1 Corinthians 13:7 says love "always trusts." Judgment, on the other hand, is condemning, and does not send the message that someone has your best interests in mind.

Judgment also creates defensiveness. Judgment can feel like an attack, and when people feel attacked, they tend to become preoccupied with justifying themselves and become angry or hostile. Relationships characterized by defensiveness certainly aren't sisterly. In fact, they tend to develop a spirit of rivalry instead (and we've talked a lot about how rivalry within the body of Christ is problematic)!

Also, James 5:16a says, "Therefore, confess your sins to each other and pray for each other so that you may be healed." Would you feel comfortable pouring out your sins and secrets to a judgmental person? No! That is another reason judgment is a big problem in relationships. It creates fear that one's information is not safe. When I feel judged, I tend to withhold information about my faults in fear that the information will be used against me. But healthy relationships, especially between close sisters in the body, are supposed to involve transparency. We are called to edify one another and pray for each other, but judgment often discourages people from being that honest and causes them to hide or only show parts of themselves in relationships.

When you start judging someone, it also biases your perspective of that person. It's as if your judgment becomes a filter through which you perceive everything about the person. If I think someone is rude, chances are I'll notice more rude things they do, I'll miss some of the kind things they do, and I may even interpret some ambiguous actions as being rude. People's thoughts and expectations tend to shape what they see. When we judge others, we are creating a bias that causes us to perpetually see the judged person in a negative light. What good can come of that in a relationship?

Finally, one major reason why judgment is so damaging in relationships is because it goes against an important aspect of love: keep no records of wrongs. 1 Corinthians 13:5 says love "keeps no record of wrongs." Judgment encourages detailed record keeping! Those of us with naturally detailed memories may find this point challenging. I remember everything! That, of course, is an overstatement, but many people who know me have remarked that I seem to remember everything. I'll say something like, "Remember back a few years ago when that guy came to preach about forgiveness, and his wife wasn't there because she had missed the flight—he was wearing a light blue blazer?" I remember details. Many women do! Unfortunately, that also means remembering with great detail wrongs done—exact words said, who was in the room, what was going on—everything! That can be problematic when it comes to not keeping records of wrongs. In fact, when I first read that verse about not keeping records, I thought to myself, "Geez—I'm like the Queen Record Keeper!"

The Queen of Judgment

Unfortunately, record keeping is a terrible practice. It ties into judgment. The only true function of keeping a record of wrongs is for proof of guilt. It legitimizes a woman's judgment in her eyes. For instance, if I make a claim that some woman is selfish and she negates it, I can call on my list of times when she was selfish to prove her wrong. Or if I even make a negative judgment about a woman in my mind, I can keep convincing myself that my thoughts are true when I review my records about her. It can also go the other way around. Keeping a record of somebody's wrongs can lead you to judge that person! Either way, record keeping presents a very unbalanced and overly negative view of the "recorded" person. It also gives the illusion that one has enough information to judge, but as we discussed earlier, only God is omniscient. Judgment thrives where there is record keeping—and record keeping is anti-love!

THE REVERSE PROBLEM

Before we finish discussing the problems with judgment, I want to make sure we talk about one other problem: accusing people of being judgmental! I have heard more accusations about people being judgmental than I perhaps have about anything else. As I mentioned at the introduction of the chapter, many people are very quick to label others as being judgmental. It's easy to see why—accusing someone of being judgmental is a very convenient way of escaping conviction. The thought is—the problem isn't me; it's the other person who's judging me! Sometimes Christians take the heat for being judgmental simply because somebody else feels convicted. I have seen that happen many times, as much as I have seen actual judgment. For instance, say a girl asks her friend what she thinks of the new guy she's dating. If the friend replies that she doesn't think this guy is a good choice, the girl, instead of hearing the truth, may accuse her friend of being judgmental so she can continue dating the guy. It's a way to avoid correction. After all, judgment aside, truth is truth. And truth is convicting. Hebrews 4:12 says, "The word of God is living and active. Sharper than any double-edged sword, it penetrates even to dividing soul and spirit, joints and marrow; it judges the thoughts and attitudes of the heart." When you stand for truth, immature people get angry. I have seen people feel threatened by someone simply walking in the room. The person didn't say anything to anyone, nor did the person have any intentions of evaluating the spirituality of the other people there, but the mere fact that the person stands for truth puts others off. It's conviction. Now, the people of God should be gentle, and any correction given should be in love (Ephesians 4:15), but people in sin who do not wish to be corrected feel the "sharp" quality of the Word and blame it on the person who stands for it. Instead of receiving conviction, the person accuses another Christian of being sharp or judgmental, when really they are just experiencing the penetration of the Word and its conviction.

That said, it is between you and the Lord to discern your own heart, whether you are the judge, the judged, or the innocent bystander. Just realize the subtleties: don't be quick to judge, don't be too quick to label somebody else as being judgmental, and also know that sometimes when you rightly stand for truth, you may be falsely accused of being judgmental.

DETHRONING THE QUEEN OF JUDGMENT

We have discussed what judgment is, the reasons we do it, why it's a problem, and how it hinders our relationships. Hopefully that information sheds light on any judgment going on in our personal lives and prompts us to change. Let's finish the chapter off and quickly discuss some things we can do to combat the practice of judging others in our lives.

1. Change your thinking. Sometimes all we need is a little mental readjustment. After all, Romans 12:2b says, "Be transformed by the renewing of your mind." We need to be reminded of our

limits. We may have knowledge of what the Word says about how a believer should live, but we are not authorized to judge, nor do we have sufficient knowledge to even begin to judge. God is the only Judge, and we need to humbly be reminded that we are unqualified to do His job.

2. Trust God's justice. Sometimes we are tempted to judge others because we want to see our wrongdoers punished! But firstly, God says, "It is mine to avenge; I will repay" (Romans 12:19). We need to trust that God will take care of our business, and not be like Job who insulted God by claiming that He fails to punish the wicked. The Bible reminds us in Hebrews 6:10, "God is not unjust." By choosing to refrain from judging, we are demonstrating our faith in God's justice and giving Him room to execute it.

3. Judge yourself. Instead of channeling your judgment toward somebody else and heaping up your own condemnation, judge yourself and spare yourself some eternal judgment. After all, the Bible says, "At whatever point you judge the other, you are condemning yourself," but on the other hand, "If we judged ourselves, we would not come under judgment" (Romans 2:1b, 1 Corinthians 11:31).

4. Examine yourself for insecurities. Finally, before you judge somebody else, stop and think about what your motives might be. Might you be feeling jealous? Proud? Threatened? Unempowered? These are insecure feelings that often drive women to judge others. The core of the problem may not be a tendency to judge, but rather insecurity in your heart. Don't be afraid or embarrassed to be honest with yourself and the Holy Spirit. After all, we are justified by grace and need only to repent—believers need not live in shame!

Dethroning the Queen

Prayer

Dear God,

Thank You for being the Righteous Judge. I know that You are completely just, and so I put my trust in You now. Lord, I invite You to search my heart. Please forgive me for judging other women in my heart, mind, speech, or actions. I know it is not loving to judge others, and that it insults You as Judge, and only brings condemnation on myself. Please forgive me. Help me to remain humble and to remember that I, too, have shortcomings and limited knowledge, and am unqualified to judge. Also, please help me to receive correction from others, and not to pass off truthful conviction as judgment, for I know that You discipline those You love. And help me to stand for the truth, even when others don't like it and accuse me of being judgmental. Holy Spirit, dethrone the reign of Queen Judgment in my life and my relationships with other women, and thank You for hearing my prayer. In Jesus' Name, I pray. Amen.

Memory Verse

"There is only one Lawgiver and Judge, the one who is able to save and destroy. But you—who are you to judge your neighbor?"
JAMES 4:12

Reflection Questions

What qualities bother you the most in other people? (These are areas to watch for).

Do those qualities ever tempt you to judge other people?

The Queen of Judgment

What type of person might you be most likely to judge? Do you need to repent or apologize for judging anyone?

What type of woman do you tend to feel the most threatened by? Does it correlate with the type of person you are likely to judge?

What records of wrongs are you holding onto? Why?

Do you have a hard time accepting criticism? Do you ever accuse others of being judgmental?

Do you need to be more receptive to conviction? Do you need to adjust your attitude toward God's correction?

Do you trust that by relinquishing your judgment, you are making room for God's perfect justice?

Action Plan!

Choose one or two people whom you struggle with judging, and start making a habit of noting the good things about them.

CHAPTER NINE

The Queen of Exclusivity

"You are all sons of God through faith in Christ Jesus."
GALATIANS 3:26

SARAH JO AND TRISHA ARE INVITED to the sleepover, but Roxanne and Donnie are not. Only the cool kids are allowed to sit at the back of the bus. The popular girls keep others from joining their double-dutch game by singing, "Tick-tock, the game is locked! You should have been here at eight o'clock!" The corner table in the cafeteria is reserved for the cheer clique and their boyfriends only. Sororities stroll in their colors, wave their hand signs in front of bystanders, and hand select only a chosen few to bear their sacred letters. The country club extends membership by invitation only. Cliques. Factions. The Haves, the Have-Nots. Throughout history, mankind has made up all sorts of reasons to distinguish certain people and leave out others. Women have a unique tendency to this behavior. It's all part of the same problem: Queen Exclusivity!

The Queen of Exclusivity—she is one of the nastier and more prevalent of the Queen Bees. She has existed throughout world culture. The issue of exclusivity surpasses gender, race, and time. I believe exclusivity has been around since man has been on the earth. It seems in every time period and culture, there has always been some form of exclusivity—some man-made way of creating a method for distinction. It's what humans do. And when women get a hold of this issue—it's pretty ugly!

Dethroning the Queen

Can you identify with any of the examples of exclusivity from the opening? I know I can. In fact, exclusivity is one of the better known stereotypes of a Queen Bee. In movies and books, the Queen Bee always has some sort of clique, and although her friends are somewhat beneath her, they still reserve rights that all others only wish they had. To reference this movie again, *Mean Girls* depicts the exclusivity of girl-girl interactions. Regina is the head of "The Plastics" (the most popular clique at the school). The Plastics have their own table in the cafeteria and social code dictates that no one else sits there. In fact, the movie's opening (and one of my favorite scenes) shows several cliques, each with its own table. Everyone understands the social rules regarding cafeteria seating. Aside from The Plastics having their own table, Regina also has rights that the other Plastics don't have (such as being the only one who is "allowed" to wear hoop earrings).[1]

AREAS OF EXCLUSIVITY

We can be exclusive about anything, not just lunch tables and hoop earrings. In one sense, being exclusive can be very childish and immature. But often it seems adults don't outgrow high school games, they just play on a bigger scale. Exclusivity can affect everything from party invitations to group memberships—even homeowner's associations and school admissions. On a serious note, exclusivity has lent itself to some of history's most horrific crimes against humanity, such as the African slave trade and the Holocaust. Regarding spiritual matters, people can even be exclusive about ministry. For example, the disciples got a little touchy when other believers started ministering. They went to Jesus, saying, "Master, we saw a man driving out demons in your name and we tried to stop him, because he is not one of us" (Luke 9:49). Clearly, when people are prone to the problem of exclusivity, they can apply it to anything.

The Queen of Exclusivity

Exclusivity Amongst Women

Since women are, generally speaking, relational creatures, we tend to display exclusivity in our groups. How often is it that you see a huge group of female friends? It exists, but it's quite rare! I have often seen female relationships exist in pairs, as seen with best friends. I have also seen small groups of three or four. But generally, the groups stay small—as compared to males, who group together in larger numbers as seen, for instance, when men get together to play sports. Men tend to do better with co-existing than women. Again, there are always exceptions and I am certainly not trying to classify people according to gender stereotypes. But it's often the case that if there is a group of one hundred girls in one organization who all know each other, the group will be divided into about twenty to thirty smaller groups of three or four. That's not completely due to exclusivity, for it is natural to congregate with similar others. But women are not just known for forming groups, we are known for forming "cliques" as well, and the distinguishing factor between groups and cliques is exclusivity. All it takes to know the difference is to try and get in with a new circle of women. Have you ever tried it? With a clique, versus just a group, an outsider will be met not with open arms, but with apathy at best, and icy snobbery at worst.

Exclusivity also generally contains an element of superiority. For women, along with cliques comes status. In junior high school one year, the girls in our class were having such a problem getting along that some of the teachers sat all the girls down for a special meeting. We were going to meet with some of the female teachers to talk out our issues. I don't remember everything we talked about that day, but there is one thing I remember quite clearly. Toward the beginning of the meeting, a teacher asked us to describe what our interactions with each other were like, just to start breaking the ice. At first, nobody wanted to speak. Then suddenly, one of the girls popped up. Though she was new that year, she had quickly risen up through the social ranks and was generally known as the new Queen Bee in town. She stood up boldly and said something like, "Okay, this is how it is. Me and Nicole are at the top. Then, after us, is like Bridget, Trina, Candice, and Kacy. They're like the 'B' group. Then there's Michelle, Doris, and Kenya. I guess they're like the 'C' group." She went on that way until she had stratified every girl in the room, even identifying the "drifters" who had no clique, but instead were individuals who drifted in between the various groups without belonging to any of them. Then she sat down. I was floored. I couldn't believe she had the audacity to declare a fixed pecking order, and place herself at the top no less! It seemed, at the time, very gutsy and arrogant—to look at a roomful of girls and essentially say that they were each, to varying degrees, beneath her! But the funny thing was, she was kind of right. Though in reality we were all girls, none above the others, we each heeded some social order that looked a lot like what this girl had described. Hence, no one protested, and she smugly sat down. Wow.

That was quite an experience, but it beautifully illustrates the status dynamic of cliques that exists amongst groups of women. Exclusivity isn't just about locking others out of a group. It always involves some sort of power, reward, status, or privilege that is reserved only for that group.

THE ROOT OF THE PROBLEM

There is a common thread that runs between all forms of exclusivity—between the kind that bans fraternizing with "nerds" in school, and the kind that produces mass genocide in race discrimination. The underlying theme of all exclusivity is this: people creating or magnifying trivial distinctions between each other in order to reserve for certain groups or individuals some sort of reward or sense of worth and acceptance.

Where Exclusivity Comes From

When some behavior seems to exist in every culture and time period, it's often an indication that the behavior is linked to an inborn human trait in

The Queen of Exclusivity

all of us. Exclusivity points to our flesh's basic, primal need to feel important and accepted. People naturally want to feel valuable, significant, and like part of a group. That's what exclusivity does. It gives us the illusion of self-worth. If I exclude certain people from my group, then I get to feel both included and special. The same thing happens if I am accepted into an exclusive group. Gaining membership into a group that excludes others lets me feel like I have something that others don't, and that feeling gives me a sense of value, acceptance, and superiority. That's partially because without God, people understand things in the context of their opposites. They tend to understand acceptance only in the context of exclusion, and worth only in the context inferiority. The lack, in contrast, gives people a sense of substance. If people fail to tap into their worth in Christ, they will often rely on contrast-based measures like exclusivity in order to satisfy their need for importance and acceptance.

The thing is, when people don't go to God with this need, the void for worth and acceptance is still there, so they try to fill it themselves. But whenever people attempt to fill a void themselves that should be filled by God, the replacement is inferior and ultimately insufficient.

The problem with exclusivity is it only gives the illusion of self-worth. One of my favorite childhood storybooks tells the tale of little creatures that had a problem with exclusivity. The creatures all looked pretty identical except for one thing: some of them had special marks on their bellies, while the others had plain bellies. The creatures with the marks used those marks as a way to distinguish themselves above the other creatures. They even had their own bonfires and beach games from which they excluded the plain-bellied creatures. But the truth was they were all quite the same, except for the mark, which was very trivial. The specially-marked creatures magnified the importance of their marks in order to feel more important, but in reality, they were no better than the plain-bellied creatures. The little mark was only a slight external difference. The discrimination drove the plain-bellied creatures to go into a machine that put marks on their bellies. In revolt, the original specially-marked creatures went into a machine to remove the marks. After a while it wasn't about the mark, but about trying to preserve a system of Haves and Have-Nots, so the Haves could feel special. At the end of the story (when the creatures could no longer tell each other apart), they all realized they were the same.

Yes, the story about these little creatures is a little cliché, but we don't tend to grasp it in real life. Exclusivity does absolutely nothing to actually make you better than someone else. For instance, if you gain membership into a choosey sorority, it doesn't actually make you better than other girls. Real worth can only come from God. Man-made exclusivity can never replace divine value. In Jeremiah 2, it says, "My people have committed two sins: They have forsaken me, the spring of living water, and have dug their own cisterns" (Jeremiah 2:13). When we rely on man-made concepts like exclusivity for our validation, we are forsaking a true, eternal source of validation for our own, cheap, inadequate sources. Yet, so often we chase after the man-made things. We give in to what society dictates as being important, because our flesh can more easily grasp earthly, rather than eternal, things.

A Genuine Human Need?

Now, just because exclusivity is a poor method doesn't mean we don't have a legitimate need for self-worth and a sense of community. That need is still valid. The key is in looking to the "spring of living water" instead of our own "broken cisterns" (Jeremiah 2:13). In other words, we need to look to God, our Creator, for our worth and identity, instead of looking to our own man-made creations. Let's again turn our attention to the kingdom of God so we can take our cues from Him.

THE KINGDOM APPROACH

We need a godly example to follow. Let's look at the kingdom of God and see how its characteristics differ from the principles of exclusivity.

The Queen of Exclusivity

No Favoritism

Favoritism is a form of exclusivity and Romans 2:11 states plainly, "God does not show favoritism." Paul emphasizes that fact in Galatians 3:26, 27 where he says, "You are all sons of God through faith in Christ Jesus, for all of you who were baptized into Christ have clothed yourselves with Christ." Notice here God is not distinguishing between us! He is not playing any favorites. It says we are all sons (or daughters) of Christ. No one is better than the others and there aren't special people getting all the special treatment. That's why the next verse says, "There is neither Jew nor Greek, slave nor free, male nor female, for you are all one in Christ Jesus. If you belong to Christ, then you are Abraham's seed, and heirs according to the promise" (Galatians 3:28, 29). There are no favorites because we are one in Christ. When we accept Jesus, we are clothed with Christ, and that erases the various distinctions that separate us in the world.

James says, "As believers in our glorious Lord Jesus Christ, don't show favoritism" (James 2:1). Since God does not show favoritism, as a response, the people of God are not supposed to show favoritism either. When we do, for instance, by giving preferential treatment to those with more money or better clothes, James says we have "discriminated among [our]selves and become judges with evil thoughts" (James 2:4). Notice James mentions "discriminating" among ourselves. We may not all attempt to be buddy-buddy with the rich, but there are many ways that we can discriminate among ourselves, picking and choosing how we interact with people based on our own categorizations of people. When we create any distinctions that affect how we treat people, we are essentially showing favoritism and coming under judgment! But as people of God, we should not show any favoritism, just as our merciful Father does not.

Pursuit of Outsiders

Romans 12:16b says, "Do not be proud, but be willing to associate with people of low position. Do not be conceited." God always pursues the outsiders, a practice that is quite contrary to exclusivity, which involves shunning outsiders. For instance, in Matthew 10 when Jesus is sending out the disciples, He commands that they go to "the lost sheep of Israel" (Matthew 10:6). God is always seeking some redemptive plan for the despised and rejected people of the world. Jesus was always going to the lame, blind, sick, orphaned, and widowed. In an adult-dominated world, Jesus looked after the children, saying, "See that you do not look down on one of these little ones" (Matthew 18:10). And even in a large group, He is always mindful of the lonely, wandering souls. He says, "If a man owns a hundred sheep, and one of them wanders away, will he not leave the ninety-nine on the hills and go look for the one that wandered off?" (Matthew 18:12). The Lord never shuns outsiders; He always pursues them. If we are His children, we should be the same way, not being apathetic or icy toward outsiders, but pursuing and welcoming them always.

Thriving on Mass Harmony

Factions are death to the body. Cliques are contrary to its very nature, because we are exactly that: one body. As we discussed in chapter two, we depend on each other to function. 1 Corinthians 12:21 says, "The eye cannot say to the hand, 'I don't need you!' And the hand cannot say to the feet, 'I don't need you!'" There can be no exclusivity in the kingdom of God because we need each other. Think of excluding someone else as chopping off a finger! That's what we do when we form cliques and fail to include others! We are damaging our own body. 1 Corinthians 12:22, 23a says, "Those parts of the body that seem to be weaker are indispensable, and the parts that we think are less honorable we treat with special honor." Those women you dislike, the women you overlook, not only are they part of your body, but they are actually extra critical for you. I know I can testify that some of the people I wanted out of my life turned out to be the ones God used for the greatest good in my life. God made it that way on purpose. He doesn't want us to be cliquish; He wants us to be humble and welcoming. "God has combined the members of the body and has given greater honor to the parts that lacked it, so that there should be no division in the body, but that its parts should have equal concern for each other" (1 Corinthians 12:24b, 25).

Value Based on God, Not Others

The world sometimes makes it seem like our value is dependent on our relationship with other people: whom we know, who our friends are, who are family is, whom we're seen with, who loves us, etc. The world can also make it seem like our value is relative. In other words, it makes it seem like we are valuable when we are better, or prettier, smarter, or more popular than others. That is part of the appeal of exclusivity. When we get into an exclusive group, we feel somehow better than others, and if we give in to the relative value mindset, exclusivity makes us feel valuable. But remember, as we discussed in the chapter about comparison, a relative value judgment is never an accurate measure. In the kingdom of God, our value is not dependent on our relationship with other people, and it is not relative. Our value is based in our relationship with Christ alone! If we were really convinced of that fact, we'd let go of exclusivity. We will get into this concept a little more in chapter thirteen, but David says, "I praise you because I am fearfully and wonderfully made; your works are wonderful, I know that full well" (Psalms 139:14). We have inherent value because of who our Creator is! God is perfect and everything He makes is good—that means you, too!

Open Invitation

One more really important quality to note about the kingdom of God is that it is precipitated on the concept of an open invitation. Contrary to what many people may think, the kingdom of God is not exclusive! God invites everyone. That's why His command to the disciples is, "Go and make disciples of all nations, baptizing them in the name of the Father and of the Son and of the Holy Spirit" (Matthew 28:19). God wants to bring people into His family. 2 Peter 3:9b says, "He is patient...not wanting anyone to perish, but everyone to come to repentance." God invites all of us. In Luke 14:15–24, Jesus tells the parable of the great banquet, and uses it to talk about God's invitation. In the parable, a man prepares a great banquet and invites many guests, but several of them decline the invitation with various excuses. The man, then, has his servants go out into the roads and country lanes until the house is full, while those who declined get no taste of the banquet. God does not exclude anyone; He only gives us the choice to decline His invitation. That's why Jesus says, "Here I am! I stand at the door and knock. If anyone hears my voice and opens the door, I will come in and eat with him, and he with me" (Revelation 3:20). We, then, as His children, should pattern ourselves the same way, and be people who extend open invitations to others.

DETHRONING THE QUEEN OF EXCLUSIVITY

As we close this chapter about exclusivity, let's just recap some ways that we can start working toward overcoming this problem:

1. Renew your mind. The world has influenced people with its beliefs and mindsets. By studying the Word of God, we see how the world's mindsets are contrary to kingdom mindsets. The world uses exclusivity to gain value, whereas the kingdom gets its value from the Lord and instead pursues others. Now that we know differently, Romans 12:2 says, "Do not conform any longer to the pattern of this world, but be transformed by the renewing of your mind." It comes down to just letting God change our thoughts. When we learn differently, we should begin thinking, and therefore acting, differently. Meditate on the concepts of this chapter, and think about the various characteristics of the Kingdom. Then let it change and influence your mindset and actions.

The Queen of Exclusivity

2. Live by the Spirit. We've got to remember, the flesh will always desire what is contrary to the Spirit, no matter how holy you get! Galatians 5:17 says, "For the sinful nature desires what is contrary to the Spirit, and the Spirit what is contrary to the sinful nature. They are in conflict with each other, so that you do not do what you want." Our flesh will always want the riches of the world—including its social riches. Here's a quick story to illustrate what I mean. When I started college, sorority life appealed to me for many reasons. Since I grew up without sisters, I loved the idea of camaraderie. But along with the sisterhood aspect of a sorority came other perks! Sororities were cool—they were exclusive! They had social status. There was a certain appeal in the idea of wearing colors and letters that others could not. I began the process of joining a sorority, but at a certain point, I was very conflicted. I do not want to negate those with very positive Greek experiences, but what I experienced was not at all like the kingdom of God.

Ultimately, that conviction was so strong that I decided to discontinue my process of joining. At the same time, the Lord was dealing with some of my friends and me about starting Christian ministries on campus. One of them was a dance ministry, but the other was a Christian women's fellowship and Bible study group called Sisters in Spirit (SIS). SIS is about Christian sisterhood, but it deliberately was not a sorority. It turned out to be awesome to have that sisterhood. But SIS did not satisfy the fleshly part of us. It did not give us the social status that a sorority would have. SIS was formed to be inclusive and friendly—and that does not validate the flesh. However, over time as we decided to walk in the Spirit, and let God renew our minds, our taste buds were renewed as well. When you walk in the Spirit, you begin to desire what God desires. Your flesh craves bologna, but God wants to get us on filet mignon. When you do things God's way, it does not always seem appealing at first. But over time, as you walk in the Spirit and let Him change you, your desires for worldly things diminish and you crave things of the Spirit instead. So, in order to dethrone the Queen of Exclusivity, you have to choose to walk in the Spirit. "Live by the Spirit, and you will not gratify the desires of the sinful nature" (Galatians 5:16).

3. Finally, remember to connect with your worth in Christ. I truly believe this one thing can solve so many of our problems as women. Reflect on Psalms 139:14. Embrace the fact that you have eternal value because of whose creation you are, and know that your value doesn't change when you are better than someone or when you get access to things that others don't have.

Prayer

Dear Lord,

Thank You for my infinite worth in You. I am only clay and dust, but I am the work of Your hands, and am fearfully and wonderfully made. Lord, help me to understand that my value is in my relationship with You and You alone, and there is nowhere I can go away from Your presence. Help me to see that shunning others, or making distinctions between people that affect how I treat them, is not a way to find true worth. Help me also to see how unlike You cliquish and exclusive behavior is. Forgive me for anything I have done to be this way, and give me a more warm, welcoming, and friendly heart. Help me to notice the outsiders, the rejected, and the lonely, and make me be an extension of You as I reach out to them with open arms. I praise You for Your love and Your transforming power, and ask these things in Jesus' Name. Amen.

The Queen of Exclusivity

Memory Verse

"You are all sons of God through faith in Christ Jesus, for all of you who were baptized into Christ have clothed yourselves with Christ. There is neither Jew nor Greek, slave nor free, male nor female, for you are all one in Christ Jesus. If you belong to Christ, then you are Abraham's seed, and heirs according to the promise."
GALATIANS 3:26–29

Reflection Questions

Who are your friends? What types of people are they in general?

Why or how do you choose your friends?

Who do you wish you were closer to? Why?

How do you feel when you are with your group in public or social settings? Are you gleaning validation in any unhealthy way?

How often do you extend invitations to others who aren't normally a part of your group?

Dethroning the Queen

What types of people do you tend to overlook? What types of people do you tend to stay away from?

Is your mindset at all exclusive? Either way, how can you be more inclusive?

Action Plan!

This week, without being condescending or patronizing, make it a point to embrace someone whom you have either shunned or overlooked in the past. Make it a habit to look out for and notice those whom you normally wouldn't, for you need them just as they need you. Keep a journal of your positive experiences.

CHAPTER TEN

The Queen of Blab

"The tongue has the power of life and death."
PROVERBS 18:21

CAN YOU THINK OF A TIME when a woman made a snide remark about you? Can you think of a time when you made a snide remark about another woman? Ever heard gossip? Ever spread gossip? Ever put your foot in your mouth by talking too much? Probably yes. Talking—it's another thing we women are known for! It's a gender generalization, but it holds a lot of truth. Women are relational, and we talk. Thus, several of our faults come out in our talking.

Words are powerful. James 3:2 says, "If anyone is never at fault in what he says, he is a perfect man, able to keep his whole body in check." That verse says a lot for the power of words! The enemy loves when we use our words to hurt others, and since women are relational, we are prime candidates for this attack. And there are so many different ways we can sin with our words! For example, I am actually known to have a somewhat reserved personality—I'm not usually the one doing most of the talking in any given situation. Small talk irritates me, and I'd rather wait until I have something important to say than say a lot of nothing. That said, even I've been very guilty of this Queen Bee quality! She creeps up on many of us! So, in this chapter, we're going to talk about the Queen of Blab and the various ways she shows up in our talking habits and damages our relationships.

Dethroning the Queen

Types of Blab

Slander

One of the blabbing sins is slander. *The New International Webster's Concise Dictionary* defines *slander* as, "The uttering of false statements or misrepresentations which defame and injure the reputation of another."[1] Notice the different elements in this definition of slander. First, it's dishonest. Secondly, it injures someone else's reputation. So put plainly, slander is any false talk that gives someone else a bad rap. Also notice the definition says "false statements or misrepresentations." This means on the one hand, slander can be lying about someone, but on the other hand, slander can be composed of statements that are, in fact, true, but are still sinful because they show a disproportionate amount of a woman's bad side. So slandering someone can also mean presenting true statements in a way that attempts to give others a negative impression of the person.

The Bible constantly commands us not to slander one another. James 4:11 is a very straightforward example: "Brothers, do not slander one another." Slander is extremely harmful, is unloving, and is a part of Queen Blab we should avoid.

Gossip

We all know gossip is wrong. Even people in the world can admit gossip is a guilty pleasure. In 2 Corinthians 12:20, Paul expresses his deep reluctance to visit Corinth because he fears there will be certain sins still prevalent amongst them, including gossip. There are various problems with gossip that we will discuss later in this chapter, but first let's discuss what gossip is. The dictionary defines *gossip* as "mischievous or idle talk, usually about the affairs of others."[2] Gossip is talking about other people in an inappropriate manner. It can be "mischievous," for instance, if we are guiltily prying into juicy secrets or scandals. Or it can be "idle," when we are simply talking about other people's private lives that do not concern us. An important quality to note about gossip is it is not necessarily mean-spirited. Speech is qualified as gossip when it is inappropriately or unnecessarily about someone else's life. So beware—gossip is not always spilling a secret about somebody else's shocking love affair. Any excessive talk about something that does not concern you is gossip!

Idle or Godless Speech

When we say someone is idle, it means they aren't doing anything productive. Idle speech is talk that is useless. It does nothing good. It's unproductive. It's only worthless sound that passes time. The Bible calls it idle, empty, or godless chatter. It involves speaking words that don't edify and lack worth or truth. Yet, people can be very caught up and even interested in idle chatter. Why else are tabloids and shallow magazines so popular? Sometimes chatty people get into idle speech. They like to talk, so they say more than is worth saying. Have you ever heard a useless conversation? Two people talking about something that may even be interesting, but is completely unproductive. Paul warns Timothy about this type of speech repetitively. In 1 Timothy 6:20, Paul urges Timothy to "turn away from godless chatter and the opposing ideas of what is falsely called knowledge." Idle chatter is a major Queen Blab quality that we should look out for!

Unwholesome Talk

Ephesians 4:29 says, "Do not let any unwholesome talk come out of your mouths, but only what is helpful for building others up according to their needs, that it may benefit those who listen." There are many types of unwholesome talk, but in this verse, unwholesome talk is contrasted with speech that benefits others and builds them up. That means there are even more types of inappropriate blab, other than slander, gossip, and even idle talk. Some common examples amongst women are tactlessness and excessive criticism. Neither one is helpful. Neither builds up. These types of speech only annoy, irritate, offend, and discourage. For example, I knew a girl in high school who always imposed her own personal style on other people's choices of clothes, shoes, or bags. If I were shopping and stopped to admire an outfit I liked, she would walk up and say, "Ew, I don't like it!" Or if another girl showed up with a brand new purse that was not to her liking, she would make a face, or express some sort of verbal disapproval. That is an example of lacking tact. It is one thing if someone asks your opinion, but if a woman is comfortable with herself and her style, it is tacky to express disapproval. Why? Because it is not helpful, and it can be very offensive. I believe tactlessness, which some purport to be mere honesty, is definitely an example of unwholesome talk. Just because something is "true" doesn't make it wholesome to speak about. Furthermore, excessive criticism or nagging can become judgment (and we discussed that Queen Bee quality in chapter eight). We are not in charge of judging and reshaping everyone else's character (as I often must remind myself since I am somewhat of a perfectionist)! That is God's job, not ours. We should beware of these types of speech, which may appear to be honest and harmless, but may actually be "unwholesome talk" that does nothing to build.

SUMMING UP THE CONCEPT OF BLAB

Slander, gossip, idle chatter, and other forms of unwholesome talk are major speech flaws that can show themselves in a wide range of behaviors. This includes lying about others, falsely accusing, misrepresenting another, orally defaming someone, fishing for information, telling secrets, talking too much, talking over others, talking more than listening, talking about nothing, swearing, entertaining unfruitful conversation, complaining about someone to a third party, saying everything you think, speaking harshly, lacking tact, nagging, and excessively criticizing. Whew! There are so many to look out for, it's no wonder this problem is so difficult for us to avoid, even when we believe our intentions to be noble. Yet there is hope, for God empowers us to be like Him in every area, and the Bible gives us the confidence to say, "I can do everything through [Christ] who gives me strength" (Philippians 4:13).

HOW WE END UP BLABBING

There are many reasons why we blab. Sometimes we blab because we are seeking validation. This used to be a big problem for me. If I felt offended and didn't know what to do, I would talk to someone else about the person who offended me in order to rally support. That kind of thing usually turns into slander, even when we don't mean it to. Women can be prone to this since we are relational. When we have a problem, we want to discuss it—but discussing our complaint with another person usually turns into slander.

Sometimes we blab intentionally (which is a particularly nasty Queen Bee characteristic). It can be a product of hatred, discord, or sheer cruelty. Other times we use our words to harm others as a form of punishing them for an offense. Another word for that is revenge. We see this on the playground. Janie says something to hurt Monica's feelings, and Monica makes a biting comment toward Janie in return. But it is never our job to punish someone by using words as an attack. Intentionally injuring someone with our words is a terrible Queen Bee sin.

Another reason might be a lack of discipline—we haven't learned how to control what we say. The key word is control. Blabbing can be an outgrowth of good qualities, such as being naturally inquisitive or very conversational. But any good quality uncontrolled or unbridled can become a problem or even a sin. Sometimes we lack discipline in the area of discernment. We fail to distinguish healthy curiosity from nosiness, and then unbridled curiosity leads to idle chatter or gossip. Other times we haven't trained ourselves to practice discretion: when, how, to whom, and how much to speak. Or, we may lack discipline in choosing our words and end up speaking tactlessly. Lack of discipline can be a major cause of blab.

Dethroning the Queen

Sometimes we even blab when we are trying to help. That's how we can end up practicing excessive criticism or even nagging. We make it our business to fix someone, or we make it our business to know about someone else's affairs so we can pray for that person. But it is often not our place to make other people's business our business.

Another way blabbing can happen is when talking with friends. We think since we are privy to our friend's information, we must be privy to the information of any person who comes into contact with our friend. For instance, I was on the phone with a certain guy, and I became a little upset about some things he was saying. My friends saw my reaction to the phone call, and pressed me to tell them what he was saying. But I refused. He had done me no harm, and at the end of the conversation we had come to an agreement. I knew that sharing the conversation would only make him look bad. My friends thought they had a right to know, since I was their friend. But even though they were my close friends, it wasn't their business, and no further help with the situation was needed. We cannot tell our friends compromising information about someone else when it's not useful simply because they are our friends—it's gossip!

THE EFFECTS OF BLAB

Here are some of the ways blabbing affects others—and even ourselves!

1. It divides. Proverbs 16:28 says, "A gossip separates close friends." I have seen it happen in my own relationships. Gossip can destroy even the closest friendships.
2. It destroys trust. Proverbs 11:13 says, "A gossip betrays a confidence." It is very difficult to trust people who talk idly about others, and all healthy relationships require trust.
3. It stirs up discord. Proverbs 26:20b says, "Without gossip a quarrel dies down." Often, gossip amplifies issues that would have otherwise gone away, promoting dissention instead of harmony.

The Queen of Blab

4. It corrupts. James 3:6 says, "The tongue also is a fire, a world of evil among the parts of the body. It corrupts the whole person, sets the whole course of his life on fire, and is itself set on fire by hell." Sinful speech can both corrupt and condemn the speaker!
5. It tears down. As you can see, Proverbs states how detrimental words can be. Proverbs 11:11 says, "Through the blessing of the upright a city is exalted, but by the mouth of the wicked it is destroyed." Ungodly speech is very damaging!
6. It leads to ungodliness. Paul warns Timothy about this in 2 Timothy 2:16, saying, "Avoid godless chatter, because those who indulge in it will become more and more ungodly." Beware of uttering or entertaining any kind of unwholesome speech—it draws people away from godliness!
7. It drives people away. Nagging and quarrelsome speech (which women are often known for) especially drive people away. It drives away friends, and even spouses. Proverbs 19:13 says, "A quarrelsome wife is like a constant dripping," and Proverbs 21:9 says, "Better to live on a corner of the roof than share a house with a quarrelsome wife."

WHY THE EMPHASIS ON WOMEN?

While the Bible addresses both genders with regard to this issue, Scriptures seem to make a particular case about women avoiding ungodly speech. In his letter to Titus, Paul emphasizes what should be specifically taught to the different genders and age groups. Titus 2:3 says, "Teach the older women to be reverent in the way they live, not to be slanderers." And in 1 Timothy 3:11, where Paul is instructing Timothy about the standards for overseers and deacons, he says, "In the same way, their wives are to be women worthy of respect, not malicious talkers but temperate and trustworthy in everything." King Solomon really nails this concept when he says, "Like a gold ring in a pig's snout is a beautiful woman who shows no discretion" (Proverbs 11:22). Yikes!

Clearly, there is something very crucial about women being godly in their speech. Personally, I believe that is for two reasons. For one, women are relational and are more prone to chatting, thus making us automatically more susceptible to talking-related sins. But more importantly, women are made to be life-giving creatures (as evidenced by our very biological makeup), and I believe we also have life-giving power in our words. Consider this: a word of encouragement can do wonders for someone's confidence and drive to achieve, while a harsh word can cut someone down. Proverbs 15:4a says, "The tongue that brings healing is a tree of life." That's the life-giving power of words. I believe God wants us to use our feminine nature and the power of words to bring life, and not abuse the gift of speech with meaningless or harmful blab.

Ways to Combat the Queen of Blab

We've discussed the many vices of Queen Blab and how those things negatively impact others and ourselves. Hopefully, describing the various types of blab has enlightened you about some areas you may need to work on. As we close this chapter, let's review some things we can do to combat the Queen of Blab in our lives:

1. Rely on God as your just Defender. When we are hurt or offended, it is natural to seek validation, comfort, and support from friends. But too often, that means defaming the person who offended us, which is slander. Instead of looking to other people to defend us, look to God. Proverbs 23:11 portrays God as our "Defender." He is the one who takes up our case. And as we learned in chapter eight (judgment), God's justice is perfect. We can trust Him with our offenses, for He cares for us.

2. Know when to suppress curiosity. Suppressing curiosity is an

important part of discretion. The root word for "discretion" is "discreet," and the dictionary definition of the word "discreet" is, "showing consideration of the privacy or trust of others, as by suppressing curious inquiry."[3] Just because we are interested in knowing something doesn't mean we should know about it. Know when something is none of your business! It will help keep you away from gossip and idle chatter.

3. Speak directly to the subject. Matthew 18:15 says, "If your brother sins against you, go and show him his fault, just between the two of you." Sometimes we get into gossip because we are discussing our business with other people, rather than with the actual subject. Although this can be difficult for non-confrontational personality types, learn to do it. It is better to be up front than to have gossip ruin a relationship. And I can attest that God can teach you how to speak up to someone when you need to!

4. Practice gentle truth-telling. We talked about needing to hold back our speech, but sometimes honest confrontation is necessary. When it is, Ephesians 4:15 encourages "speaking the truth in love." Often it is not what you say, but how you say it. When I have a bone to pick with someone, I often find myself complaining about the person's tone, rather than their actual words, and vice versa. Proverbs 15:1 says, "A gentle answer turns away wrath, but a harsh word stirs up anger." Sometimes gentleness is the key to avoiding sin in our speech. That can be difficult when we are upset or passionate, but it is the godly way to behave. After all, learning to be gracious is important, particularly for women. I like the way the King James Version puts it— "A gracious woman retaineth honour" (Proverbs 11:16, KJV).

5. Listen before you speak and listen more than you speak. James 1:19 says, "Everyone should be quick to listen, slow to speak."

Dethroning the Queen

Have you ever witnessed people who talk before they have the facts? People who are quick to speak end up making fools of themselves much of the time. Plus, they tend to be obnoxious, as well. Proverbs 29:20 says, "Do you see a man who speaks in haste? There is more hope for a fool than for him." To avoid being this way, make sure you listen first, both to others and to God. And as James 1:19 encourages, try to do more listening than speaking.

6. Speak only useful words. Remember the wisdom in Ephesians 4:29, which says, "Do not let any unwholesome talk come out of your mouths, but only what is helpful for building others up according to their needs, that it may benefit those who listen." Test your words. Consider how many of them are helpful and how many are not. Practice giving life by only speaking words that edify.

7. Monitor how much you talk. Proverbs 10:19a says, "When words are many, sin is not absent." Have you ever been up late talking, and pretty soon you could sense the conversation getting pointless or even ungodly? That's because when there's nothing left to say, we need to stop talking! Too often we try to fill silence with unnecessary words. But excessive talk promotes sin—and since there are so many tongue-related sins, scaling back on how much you talk is not a bad idea! Consider the wisdom in Proverbs 11:12, which reads, "A man who lacks judgment derides his neighbor, but a man of understanding holds his tongue."

8. Institute some speech checks. It's not just about suppressing your self-expression, because there is value in words. It's about practicing discernment and discretion: knowing when to talk, whom to speak to, what to say, and how much to say it! It's about asking the Holy Spirit to help you control your speech.

The Queen of Blab

James 3:3 says, "When we put bits into the mouths of horses to make them obey us, we can turn the whole animal." Think of your mouth as a horse. It wouldn't be wise to try to get to a destination by riding a wild horse without a bridle! How would you direct it? How would you keep it from running amok? Well the same goes for our mouths. Talking can certainly be very valuable, but if there is no bridle, nothing that imposes restraint or checks our words, our mouths can run wild and get us into big trouble.

9. Walk in the Spirit. If you hadn't noticed, walking in the Spirit is the key to dethroning any type of sin. Unwholesome speech such as slander and gossip are products of the flesh (Colossians 3:8), but Galatians 5:16 says, "Live by the Spirit, and you will not gratify the desires of the sinful nature." Also, when we walk in the Spirit, the Spirit bears fruit in our lives. One of those fruits is self-control, as we see in Galatians 5:23. The Spirit will help us put to death our sinful nature and learn to exhibit self-control in every area, including our speech! If we can learn to control our speech, we will stay far away from the types of Queen Bee comments that make our skin crawl, and we'll have healthier, more harmonious relationships!

Prayer

Heavenly Father,
Thank You for Your Word, which is always helpful and edifying. Thank You for desiring to purify my speech to be holy, just as Your Word is holy. I ask forgiveness now for every unfruitful, hurtful, or idle word I've spoken. Teach me how to not be at fault in what I say. Give me wisdom, discernment, discretion, graciousness, and gentleness in my speech. May what I say make me sound like You. Cleanse my mouth and control my tongue. Make my mouth an agent of healing, not tearing down. I will follow Your Holy

Dethroning the Queen

Spirit and allow You to change me in this area. And I know You will help me to improve. I ask these things in Jesus' Name and thank You for what You are going to transform. Amen.

Memory Verse

"Do not let any unwholesome talk come out of your mouths, but only what is helpful for building others up, according to their needs, that it may benefit those who listen."
EPHESIANS 4:29

Reflection Questions

Review the various types of blab discussed at the beginning of the chapter (slander, gossip, etc.). Which of them surprised you or made you think? Where are your areas of weakness?

When seeking information about a person or situation, do you consider the other person's privacy and the appropriateness of your involvement?

Do you speak first or listen first? Which do you do more?

To whom do you talk when you have a problem with someone?

What do you talk about the most?

The Queen of Blab

Take a survey of your words. Are most of them helpful and edifying? Idle, meaningless, and empty? Damaging, insulting, or hurtful?

How do people react to your talking? What does that tell you?

How often do you talk about other people? (Even if it's not malicious).

What are the speaking habits of the people you are closest to?

Based on your answers and the concepts in this chapter, what can you do to improve your speaking?

Action Plan!

Today, try an experiment. Every time you open your mouth, make sure the words are helpful and beneficial in some way. If they are not, hold your tongue. Have someone keep you accountable about it today. Take note of what kinds of comments you suppress and see if it gives you any insight into your speaking habits and what you need to work on.

CHAPTER ELEVEN

The Queen of Subtext

"Help, Lord, for the godly are no more...
Everyone lies to his neighbor; their flattering lips speak with deception."
PSALMS 12:1, 2

I SIMPLY LOVE THE TOPIC OF SUBTEXT. It's so real, yet so hidden. I love bringing the beast out from under the surface for everyone to see! Subtext—we've all experienced it. Hints. Loaded comments. The stuff between the lines. Implications. Suggestions. Everything spoken, or even unspoken, that has a hidden but very perceivable message.

Many women are masters of subtext. We know how to say something without saying it. Sometimes we even know how to convey something while saying the opposite. We can turn a simple hello into a secret, "I hate you!" In the hands of a woman, a seemingly innocent comment can be a merciless attack. We know when it happens to us. Everything she said seemed fine on the surface, but somehow we feel cut, degraded, and insulted! When that happens, we've been victims of subtext.

When we talk about subtext, we are talking about underlying meaning. A woman can say one thing and mean another. That's the entire concept of subtext. It's being able to communicate something without having to actually say it. It's more biting that way, many would argue. It stings worse when your enemy can cut you with a smile on her face. It adds insult to injury. It's a slap in the face, because the person can insult you and get away with it (since subtext is all under the surface). It's the girl version of a sucker punch!

Uses of Subtext

What are some ways women use subtext? One way is to pass off insults or criticisms. Say you are out with a group of women, and there is one woman there whom you don't particularly care for. You might casually say to one woman, "I love your dress! It's so pretty, yet modest. It's a true sign of beauty when a woman can look attractive without flaunting her body." That could be a genuine compliment. But if the woman you don't like is within earshot, and you are trying to make her feel bad for wearing a miniskirt, then your compliment of the one woman is really a masked attack of the other. That's one example of subtext. Subtext can even happen in church! Say you are sitting near a woman who, for instance, is living with her boyfriend. You don't like her. So when the pastor starts talking about shacking up and fornication, you say a loud, "Amen!" If you say that for the woman to hear, it's subtext! You are acting like you are merely supporting the pastor's good teaching, when really you are trying to make the woman next to you feel bad about herself. That's the wickedness of subtext. It can happen in any setting and in many ways.

Sometimes women use subtext to manipulate other women. Manipulation is when someone attempts to control someone else deceitfully. Say you want a certain woman to pitch in more when organizing a community event. When she is your presence, you might say something like, "This community is so great, but unfortunately it's not as good as it could be since people don't assume leadership." That's subtext. It's also manipulative. You are trying to influence her to feel guilty and take action. But you are passing off this attempt as general conversation. It's a veiled comment. That makes it not just controlling, but also deceitful, which combines to make it manipulative.

The Queen of Subtext

Here's another nasty way women can use subtext: secretly one-upping another woman. You often see this between women who are competing. It's like an underground battle. I like an example from which movie? You've got it—*Mean Girls*. At one point in the movie, Cady starts liking Regina's ex-boyfriend, Aaron. Although Regina says she doesn't mind, she gets jealous of Cady and gets back with Aaron to spite her. Here's an excerpt from that scene:

> **Regina [to Aaron]:** "Why do you wear your hair like that? Your hair looks so sexy pushed back. Cady, will you please tell him his hair looks sexy pushed back?"
>
> **Cady [narrating her thoughts]:** "Regina was dangling Aaron in front of me on purpose. I knew how this would be settled in the animal world." [She pictures herself pouncing on Regina in a cat-fight]. "But this was Girl World."
>
> **Cady [to Aaron]:** "Your hair looks sexy pushed back."
>
> **Cady [narrating her thoughts]:** "And in Girl World, all the fighting had to be sneaky."[1]

This scene picks up on the subtleties of subtext, and how it can be used to one-up someone else. Regina was acting like she was merely paying Aaron a compliment, but she was actually using it as an opportunity to flaunt Aaron in front of Cady. She wanted to rack up a point for herself against Cady. Cady picks up on the maliciousness behind Regina's seemingly innocent comment by noting that in the animal world, that interaction would have been a vicious fight, like a scrap between two lionesses. Yet, in "girl world," the fighting was "sneaky." It wasn't done with claws, it was done with underhanded comments. That's how subtext can work. We can use our seemingly innocent speech to imply something that slights someone else, or that gives us a leg up in our never-ending verbal brawls.

Why We Use Subtext

Why do women use subtext? Are we just so cruel that we want our offenses to have the extra sting of mocking flattery? There are several reasons why a woman might use subtext. Let's look at a few.

Insecurity

People who constantly need to engage in verbal wars or put someone else down are often insecure. Subtext can be a sign that the person feels inadequate in some way, and seeks to gain something out of making someone else feel bad.

Pride or Competition

We will talk about pride in the next chapter, but sometimes we use subtext out of one-upmanship. That desire for status or prestige, and the desire to out-do someone else, comes from Queen Competition (remember chapter four!). Competitive women may use subtext, failing to see how they are being prideful (or perhaps even insecure).

Judgment

Sometimes we use subtext self-righteously. We want someone to feel bad about a certain behavior we don't approve of, so we express our disapproval in subtext, or use subtext to bring a sense of conviction upon the person. When we use subtext this way, we are becoming judgmental and manipulative. It is not our duty to control someone else's convictions; it is God's.

Desire to control

Some people struggle with a desire to control others. Certain personality types may be susceptible to this habit, such as leaders or perfectionists. They want others to conform to their expectations, and will resort to subtle persuasion or manipulation. These individuals may be unaware that their actions are stemming from an unhealthy attempt to control others.

The Queen of Subtext

Cruelty

Sometimes as women we just want to put the extra sting in our offenses out of spite. Subtext can be used to both insult someone and mock the person by smiling while hurting her. It's part of "girl world." Being able to get away with a biting comment is a thrill for spiteful people, or those with cruel intentions.

Cowardice

Women don't always use subtext out of cruelty. Another reason women may use subtext is because of cowardice—they are afraid to come out and say what they think to another woman. Women who are non-confrontational may resort to subtext in order to get their point across. Despite the lack of maliciousness, this can still be a problem, as we will see in this next section.

THE OTHER KIND OF SUBTEXT: ATTEMPTING TACT

I want to be sure I mention another type of subtext as well. It is really the same problem, but it comes from a completely different motive. Some women believe using subtext is more tactful than having to directly confront someone. Similar to cowardice, this motive also lacks malicious intent. Yet it's still problematic. Trust me, I used to use this kind of subtext when I wanted to say something without creating a confrontation. It's always a big problem—let's look at why.

Problems With Tact-driven Subtext

Sometimes we think using subtext is a gentler way of correcting someone, but I can attest that such thinking is untrue! Here's a personal example of mine. Once, in college, I got very angry with one of my friends who had offended me. In my frustration, and lack of confrontation, I talked about the situation to someone else. That was a mistake; I should have just gotten some guts and spoken directly to the person I was upset with, but I didn't. Apparently another friend overheard me discussing the matter behind the girl's back. So the next day, when we were all together, the one who overheard made an announcement in front of the group. She merely recited a Bible verse about gossip, and then sat down. I picked up on what she was doing and was annoyed, as well as a little defensive, and asked her why she read the verse. She responded that she merely felt it was a good verse to share. Now, the truth was, I had been gossiping. For her to think the verse applied was completely right. However, she didn't say it directly to me. She said it indirectly—and to an entire group of people. She used subtext, and it offended me. I was wrong, but her statement didn't prompt me to apologize. Instead, I felt sneakily attacked in front of a group. Subsequently, our group began to experience dissention. This whole situation became a big web of issues, such as confronting gossip, which we eventually straightened out. But one of the many things I learned in that situation was about the attempt to correct people with subtext.

Subtext doesn't come off right. It just doesn't. I used to use subtext a lot because I thought it was gentler than direct confrontation. I thought it gave the person a chance to correct her behavior without being directed or pinpointed. Right? Wrong! Subtext almost always feels crueler than confrontation. People feel manipulated when they are corrected with subtext. A person who uses subtext has a secret agenda. Her intentions aren't clear. Even when the person has good intentions, there seems to be something malicious about the use of subtext. After all, what well-intended person ever had to hide? There's something about it that seems shifty. People tend not to trust the unknown. With a loaded comment or innuendo, the person's agenda remains unknown, leading to distrust. When the speaker remains in the shadows, you wonder what dubious intentions she has.

All I am saying is that while subtext may seem like a tactful way of correcting someone (as it used to seem to me), it can definitely come off as an offense. I didn't realize that until it happened to me. Tact involves careful wording, not deceptive speech or double-talk with hidden meaning. I've made that mistake plenty of times. The response has almost always been glaringly negative. People are insulted when they feel someone has tried to secretly, yet obviously, chide them. It's just a bad idea, however innocently intended.

OTHER PROBLEMS WITH SUBTEXT

There are several other problems with subtext as well. It is the underground tension that causes earthquakes and volcanoes. Have you ever witnessed a subtext war? Have you seen two people not get along, but never come out and say anything directly? These problems always tend to be magnified. Unspoken issues leave a lot of room for assumption, misinterpretation, exaggeration, and resentment. All of these factors can play a part in magnifying a problem. Plus, there is less opportunity to resolve an unspoken issue. It is easy to deny and therefore difficult to address. As a result, these issues can be some of the most colossal.

Another problem with subtext is that it gives the person an excuse to dodge even a valid correction. People are defensive creatures. The more immature a person is, the more she will want to fight any correction. Our flesh doesn't like it at all. Subtext is an ineffective tool for people who have genuine complaints, because an immature person will negate the complaint on the basis that it was not presented to her face. Don't give people another reason to dodge what you are saying. If the person is already touchy, don't add insult to injury by masking your correction. It will only give the person an excuse to make the problem about you and not about them.

A huge problem with subtext is its manipulative quality. Manipulation is scary. While it may not seem serious, it is often likened to witchcraft! The definition of "witchcraft" is, "Black magic," or magic empowered by evil forces.[2] Magic, in turn, is defined as, "Any supernatural power or control over natural laws or the forces of nature."[3] Both manipulation and witchcraft have this in common: an attempt to exert some sort of unnatural control over someone else. As women, we should be very careful that we don't try to control people with our words—it is very evil and ungodly!

Finally, perhaps the biggest problem with subtext is expressed in Psalms. David cries out to God, saying, "Help, Lord, for the godly are no more... Everyone lies to his neighbor; their flattering lips speak with deception. May the Lord cut off all flattering lips and every boastful tongue" (Psalms 12:1–3). David, here, expresses distress over deceptive speech. That's essentially what subtext is. It is speech that appears to be one thing, but is actually another, and when we engage in deceptive speech, we do two things: we become ungodly, and we also create distrust amongst others. In essence, we damage our relationship with God, and we damage our relationship with other people. Deception is not Christ-like. In Psalms 15:1–3, David says, "Lord, who may dwell in your sanctuary? Who may live on your holy hill? He whose walk is blameless and who does what is righteous, who speaks the truth from his heart and has no slander on his tongue, who does his neighbor no wrong and casts no slur on his fellowman." That section is all about speech! Truth is godly, while slander and spiteful innuendos like "slur" are ungodly. The deceptive element of subtext can destroy trust, which is critical for healthy, loving relationships.

Tips for Dethroning the Queen of Subtext

This chapter is not about reading other women's subtext, because how can you know someone else's thoughts? Don't start reading into every woman's comments. This chapter is about you. You can only break the cycle by making sure you are not being a Queen of Subtext. Based on what we have learned about subtext in this chapter, here are some things we can practice to continue to combat it in our lives:

1. Say what you mean. Proverbs 27:5 says, "Better is open rebuke than hidden love." Sometimes the truth hurts, but subtext is untrustworthy, and ends up doing much more long-term dam-

age. Remember Proverbs 27:6: "Wounds from a friend can be trusted, but an enemy multiplies kisses."

2. Examine your heart for insecurities or other Queen Bee issues that could be prompting you to injure others with subtext. Pride, competition, antipathy, jealousy, and slander all lend themselves to the use of subtext. Dealing with these may help you deal with subtext.

3. Let God be in control. Don't try to manipulate others. Let God be the Judge. He is the One in charge of other people. Relinquish your habit of attempting to criticize, manipulate, or control others with subtext. Other women must answer to God, not to you!

4. Monitor your speech. The same principles from chapter ten (Queen of Blab) apply here. Remember Ephesians 4:29, "Do not let any unwholesome talk come out of your mouths, but only what is helpful for building others up according to their needs, that it may benefit those who listen." Check your words. Make sure they are bringing truth and life!

Prayer

Dear Lord,

Thank You that You are a God of truth and honesty. You are gentle, but firm, gracious, yet honest. Teach me to be more like You. Lord, forgive me for the times when I used deceptive speech to control, injure, or one-up another woman. I realize my use of subtext and underlying meanings is not loving or trustworthy, and it is not a reflection of You. Lord, please give me the boldness to say what I need to say, the honesty to say it in a straightforward manner, and the gentleness to speak the truth in a way that is loving and receivable. I want to be a woman who is known for godly speech, not a deceptive, flattering tongue. Thank You, Holy Spirit, for dethroning the Queen of Subtext in my life, and I pray for better

Dethroning the Queen

communication with my sisters in Christ. I ask these things in Jesus' Name and thank You for what You are going to do. Amen.

Memory Verse

"Better is open rebuke than hidden love. Wounds from a friend can be trusted, but an enemy multiplies kisses."
PROVERBS 27:5, 6

Reflection Questions

Are you more confrontational or non-confrontational?

Are you straightforward with people?

Are you ever controlling?

Have you ever attempted to insult anyone indirectly? Who? Why?

When you feel someone is trying to one-up you in a conversation, does it bother you? How do you respond? Do you ignore it? Do you entertain the person? Do you use subtext in response?

The Queen of Subtext

Do you say what you mean?

Are your words trustworthy? Are they ever deceptive or misleading?

Action Plan

Identify someone whom you tend to use subtext with. Ask the Holy Spirit how to go about addressing the hidden issues. If you have a problem controlling others, pray that you would be able to release those issues to God's control, and write down what you are releasing to Him.

CHAPTER TWELVE

The Queen of Pride

*"Do nothing out of selfish ambition or vain conceit, but
in humility consider others better than yourselves."*
PHILIPPIANS 2:3

OUR LAST QUEEN BEE CHARACTERISTIC to dethrone is the Queen of
Pride. Pride is one of mankind's deepest-rooted sins. *The New International
Webster's Concise Dictionary* defines *pride* this way: "An undue sense of one's
own superiority; arrogance; conceit."[1] Pride can manifest in many ways.
The word "sense" implies pride can be both a hidden, internal trait, as well
as an outward display. For instance, pride can be thinking too much of
oneself. It can take the form of believing oneself to be better than others.
Or it can be behaving in a way that is inappropriate for one's status (doing
something that would suggest you are better than others, even if this is not
your conscious thought). We will discuss the various ways pride manifests
later. But pride seems to be a fundamental characteristic of the flesh. It is
quite arguable that sin entered the world by the vehicle of pride. This is a
very important concept, so let's take a moment to look at it closer.

THE ENTRY OF PRIDE INTO THE WORLD

Satan's existence was, in a way, precipitated by his pride. Satan was originally the angel, Lucifer. Ezekiel 28 tells the story. It talks about how Lucifer
was anointed as a guardian angel, and how he was initially blameless until,
as God says to him, "Wickedness was found in you" (Ezekiel 28:15).

Dethroning the Queen

Lucifer had the potential to sin, and became full of pride. In Isaiah 14, God says this of him: "You said in your heart, 'I will ascend to heaven; I will raise my throne above the stars of God; I will sit enthroned on the mount of assembly, on the utmost heights of the sacred mountain. I will ascend above the tops of the clouds; I will make myself like the Most High'" (Isaiah 14:13, 14). Lucifer became haughty. His desire to be like God, and assume God's place, was arrogant and deeply prideful. As a result of his sinful pride, Lucifer could no longer exist in heaven and was cast out. God says, "So I threw you to the earth; I made a spectacle of you before kings" (Ezekiel 28:17b). So pride was the sin that originally caused the angel Lucifer to become the Devil Satan. Sin is sin; I don't mean to make any one sin out to be worse than the others. But this story ought to tell you something about the seriousness and danger of pride!

The story doesn't end there. Man also sinned. That story is told in Genesis. Eve sinned when she ate some of the forbidden fruit. She sinned because the serpent, the devil, deceived her (Genesis 3:1, 13). (Deception is a crucial problem to look out for!) But notice what the serpent deceives her about. God had commanded Adam and Eve, "You are free to eat from any tree in the garden; but you must not eat from the tree of the knowledge of good and evil, for when you eat of it you will surely die" (Genesis 2:16, 17). The serpent challenges God's command when he talks to Eve, and he says, "God knows that when you eat of it your eyes will be opened, and you will be like God, knowing good and evil" (Genesis 3:5). The serpent tempted Eve with the idea of becoming "like God," which is prideful. Eve then looked at the fruit, desired it and the knowledge that would come from eating it, and ate some (Genesis 3:6). There are many dimensions to this story, but what I want to emphasize for the purposes of this chapter is its relation to pride. The Devil, who himself became tempted with pride, deceived Adam and Eve into sinning by also tempting them with pride—and that incident marked the fall of man. Thus, our flesh is stamped with pride. It is embedded within our human nature.

The Queen of Pride

OTHER CAUSES OF PRIDE

We've just discussed that one of the most basic origins of pride is mere fleshly human nature. Humans are prideful beings. But there are other issues that can lead to pride as well. Here are some other contributing factors. In Ezekiel 28, the story of Lucifer's fall from heaven, God says of Lucifer, "Your heart became proud on account of your beauty, and you corrupted your wisdom because of your splendor" (Ezekiel 28:17). Here we see another precursor to pride: vanity. In other words, we can also fall into pride when we get caught up in our own beauty, talent, skill, ability, achievement, wisdom, or other assets. A healthy dose of self-esteem is very important. But excessive admiration of ourselves leads to pride. After all, that's what happened to Lucifer. The Bible describes him as a "model of perfection, full of wisdom and perfect in beauty" (Ezekiel 28:12). But he got full of himself! He looked at his own glory and became proud, and that pride ultimately caused his transformation into Satan. Wow! I am amazed at the evils that can result from pride! But notice how it happens. Lucifer, before wickedness was discovered in him, appeared to be beautiful, seemingly perfect, a model angel, one to be admired. Does that sound like anyone you know? Many Queen Bee types can be rather vain. They are full of themselves and obsess over their own virtues or assets. Beauty and wisdom were particular areas of pride for Lucifer, and I believe the same goes for us. Women, also, are naturally glorious beings. We were made to reveal and reflect beauty. Our bodies are intricate. God made us to be attractive (no matter what some women may say)! But— we have got to check vanity. I know it's hard. We can be a mix of vanity and insecurity at the same time. Both extremes are dangerous. Healthy self-esteem is the balance, but excessive self-admiration leads to pride! And based on this story, and mere personal experience, I would especially look out for vanity in the areas of beauty and wisdom. Wisdom, while being good in and of itself, just like beauty, can also lead to pride when we think too highly of our own wisdom. 1 Corinthians 8:1b, 2 says, "We

Dethroning the Queen

know that we all possess knowledge. Knowledge puffs up, but love builds up. The man who thinks he knows something does not yet know as he ought to know." Again, the Bible makes it clear that gaining wisdom, knowledge, and understanding are critical for all believers. Do not think that knowledge in and of itself is evil—I have heard many Christians erroneously claim that. Rather, pride creeps in when we become caught up in our own knowledge, failing to recognize that we are merely humans, that we don't know everything, and that the knowledge we do have comes from God.

There's one more area I want to highlight on the subject of looking out for pride: insecurity or low self-esteem! It seems ironic, possibly even contradictory, that insecurity would be a cause of pride, but it can be. People who suffer from insecurity or low self-esteem sometimes seek validation or value in an unhealthy manner (since their notion of value isn't in a healthy place to begin with). For instance, say a woman always felt overlooked in life, and since she didn't draw on her worth in Christ, being overlooked caused her to suffer from low self-esteem. Then say she started singing, and had a real talent. Other people started noticing her because she was a great singer, and so she started using her singing to gain attention. The attention validated her, so she put a lot of stock in her ability to sing, and eventually became caught up in admiring her talent because of how it made her feel. She could become prideful about her singing, because pride makes her feel good. Often, insecure people will rely on superiority for their sense of self-worth, and that superiority complex is prideful. It's a thin line, but often a person whose self-esteem is wavering can swing to the opposite extreme of pride when seeking a feeling of importance.

SIGNS OF PRIDE

Now pride does not always manifest in predictable ways. It is not merely found in those who walk around with their noses in the air. Pride is tricky!

182

The Queen of Pride

And it can be very subtle. Here are some signs that may indicate a pride issue:

1. Center of attention. Desiring the spotlight. Constantly wanting all eyes on you. If you have a tendency to desire all of the attention and fail to consider others or let them have the spotlight sometimes, you might be dealing with pride. Excessive interest in self, to the point that others are not considered or are disadvantaged, is a major problem!
2. Boasting, bragging, or flaunting. This is a more obvious demonstration of pride. If you are constantly talking about your achievements, frequently taking credit for your successes, or calling people's attention to your strengths, you may be struggling with pride.
3. Can't apologize. If you can't apologize, it's very likely you have a pride issue. Refusal to apologize sends the message that you are above error, or that you are infallible. Such thinking is definitely too lofty for any human. Furthermore, substituting explanations for apologizes, indicates pride as well. If, when presented with a criticism, you explain yourself, rather than say you are sorry, you are actually justifying yourself rather than humbling yourself. This is pride.
4. Can't give compliments. We've talked about this problem before. It comes up in other Queen Bee characteristics, such as jealousy and competition. Inability or reluctance to give compliments can also be a sign of pride. It shows an unwillingness to step off your pedestal and let someone else get praise. This is just like Lucifer. He didn't want to give God praise. He wanted all the praise for himself. Not giving compliments is a form of wanting all the praise for ourselves—and it is a very wicked form of pride!

Dethroning the Queen

5. Judgmental. The Queen Bee qualities certainly overlap. Judgment is also an indication of pride. Why? Because in judging someone, you are virtually acting like you have the ability to judge him or her in the first place. It is a gross oversight of one's own frailties and weaknesses. A humble person knows she is incapable of judging another because she, too, is flawed. When you judge someone, you are taking on the position of infallibility and supreme knowledge. This position is reserved for God, only, and when we attempt to take His place, it's pride.

6. Defensive. We touched upon defensiveness in the point about failing to apologize. But some people are always defensive, even when no one is accusing them of anything. Constantly justifying and explaining yourself is defensiveness, and again, it essentially comes from an assumption of infallibility. Most of us admit we're not perfect. Yet we'll be defensive in a heartbeat. Remember, pride can be reflected in your thoughts or your behavior. You may admit you're not perfect, but if your actions or words are defensive, you are suggesting superiority in some way. You are failing to humble yourself or admit to areas of weakness. This, too, is pride.

7. Having the last word. Always needing to have the last word is both prideful and obnoxious. It shows a severe lack of humility. Humility, the opposite of pride, is willing to bear with other people's words, even when one disagrees. But prideful people always need to overthrow someone with a last comment. It is a sign of an unwillingness to be corrected, challenged, or even spoken to. That is a major sign of pride.

8. "Deserve" mentality. Often I hear people say things like, "You deserve this," or "She doesn't deserve that," and so on. Thinking you deserve good things or don't deserve bad things is prideful! It seems contrary, doesn't it? But it's true. The truth is none of

us deserve anything. Sure, we may have done praiseworthy things in our lifetimes, or perhaps have suffered unjustly, but we have already been blessed beyond anything we could ever deserve through salvation in Christ. It's like being given a trillion dollars, simply because the giver felt generous, and then thinking you are owed a hundred more dollars. It's prideful, because it suggests we place undue importance on our deeds.

9. Selfish and/or inconsiderate. Selfishness really is its own problem, yet it is very closely related to pride, especially with regard to the concept of a Queen Bee, so we will discuss selfishness here. Selfishness is pride's sister. If you frequently put your needs above the needs of others, you are showing arrogance. Your behavior suggests you are more important than others when you aren't. Similarly, inconsideration is a huge part of selfishness, thus it's also related to pride. Inconsideration is failure to think about or show concern for other people's wishes, comfort, preferences, or well-being. Inconsideration can come from being outright dismissive of others or it can come from oversight. Either way, failure to consider others is arrogant, no matter what the reason. If you prioritized others more, you wouldn't overlook their concerns. After all, at the end of the day, people notice what they care about. Selfishness and inconsideration are major indications of arrogant pride. Selfishness and pride combined account for a very large percentage of failed and dysfunctional relationships!

THE INSUFFICIENCY OF PRIDE

The fact that pride led to the fall of Satan is pretty indicative that pride is a major ethical problem. But it's also a functional problem as well. Here are some biblical principles that outline the various issues and insufficiencies of pride:

Dethroning the Queen

Pride is Only False Worth

Sometimes people think being prideful is being strong. They think demonstrating their successes, achievements, and virtues is admirable. However, being prideful is a very hollow form of validation. Consider something Jesus says to His disciples. In John 8:54, Jesus says, "If I glorify myself, my glory means nothing. My Father, whom you claim as your God, is the one who glorifies me." When we glorify ourselves, our glory means nothing. It is natural to desire appreciation or admiration. But if we are so thirsty for these things that we become prideful, then we are defeating the purpose. It's as if pride cancels out our praiseworthiness. True praise comes not from ourselves, but from God.

Pride Will End in Humiliation

Another problem with pride is that it always gets shot down. The popular saying, "Pride goes before a fall," comes from Proverbs 16:18. The NIV version says, "Pride goes before destruction, a haughty spirit before a fall." Those who exalt themselves will be opposed and overthrown. Much of Proverbs is dedicated to that one concept. Consider the story in Luke 14 when Jesus is at a Pharisee's House. In an act of pride, many of the Pharisees chose for themselves the places of honor at the table. Jesus rebukes them, saying, "When someone invites you to a wedding feast, do not take the place of honor, for a person more distinguished than you may have been invited" (Luke 14:8). Instead, Jesus encourages this: "When you are invited, take the lowest place, so that when your host comes, he will say to you, 'Friend, move up to a better place'. Then you will be honored in the presence of all your fellow guests" (Luke 14:10). It is prideful to go somewhere and pick the best seat, or the best of anything, before being invited to do so. I know some people who always seem to rush ahead of others. They jump to the front of the line, they move in front of others when someone they want to talk to comes around. They take large portions of the food at parties or get-togethers. These aren't always signs of

The Queen of Pride

pride, but often they are. Again, it shows an undue sense of one's own importance. Who's to say you should be at the front of the line and not somebody else? Are you so much more important than others that you should get the best of everything, or a preferential seat? These are the subtleties of pride. Selfishness can also get mixed in here. But Jesus advises us not to be that way, warning us that such behavior will only result in humiliation. At the end of the story of the Pharisee's house Jesus warns, "For everyone who exalts himself will be humbled, and he who humbles himself will be exalted" (Luke 14:11).

There is another very startling example of pride ending in humiliation. God cannot stand pride. Arrogance cannot exist in His presence (which is why Lucifer's pride got him thrown out of heaven). Proverbs 16:5 says, "The Lord detests all the proud of heart. Be sure of this: They will not go unpunished." When He says that, He means it! Isaiah 3 gives a frightening example. Now it is always a good idea to tread lightly in the prophet books—they can seem pretty harsh! Isaiah was a prophet who was instructed to speak to the people of Israel, who had rebelled against God. In one section, he speaks to the women of Israel, saying, "The women of Zion are haughty, walking along with outstretched necks, flirting with their eyes, tripping along with mincing steps, with ornaments jingling on their ankles," and as a result of their arrogance, Isaiah tells them God is going to take away their jewels, finery, fine clothes, mirrors, perfumes—and even their hair to make them bald (Isaiah 3:16–26)! Yikes! Now, this was a prophesy for Israel, basically warning them that their haughtiness will bring about ruin. I don't mention this Scripture to say that if you become prideful God is going to snatch you bald! But it serves as an illustration of how much the Lord detests arrogance. It certainly puts a healthy dose of fear in me! Since we are His children, we should instead clothe ourselves with humility and let God exalt us.

Dethroning the Queen

Pride is Contrary to Love

Finally, pride hinders our relationships because it is contrary to love. There are several characteristics of love found in 1 Corinthians 13 that are contrary to pride, such as "does not boast," "is not proud," and "is not self-seeking" (1 Corinthians 13:4, 5). Arrogance suggests those around you are inferior. Selfishness implies your needs are more important than the needs of others. Pride, simply, is unloving. Unless you let the Holy Spirit dethrone the Queen of Pride, your relationships with other women (and with men) will suffer.

WHAT TO DO INSTEAD

Pride clearly is not the way, so what is? Philippians 2 gives some insight. It says, "Do nothing out of selfish ambition or vain conceit, but in humility consider others better than yourselves" (Philippians 2:3). The key is humility. Here is the definition of the word *humble*: "Having or expressing a sense of selflessness, meekness, modesty, etc. Lowly in condition, rank, etc.; unpretending."[1] Humility is about accepting a low position in order to focus, instead, on the needs and well-being of other people. Human nature tells us to look out for ourselves first. God tells us to look out for others first, and let Him be the one to look out for us.

The next verse in Philippians explains this concept even further, saying, "Each of you should look not only to your own interests, but also to the interests of others" (Philippians 2:4). In other words, choose to be more cognizant of other people's welfare. We are trained to be aware of our own interests. But remember, we are not just individuals; we are a part of a body. We need to look out for the interests of the entire body then, as well. We need to be aware and concerned about others, and not put ourselves ahead of them.

Paul commands us to be like Christ, "Who, being in very nature God, did not consider equality with God something to be grasped, but made himself nothing, taking the very nature of a servant, being made in human

The Queen of Pride

likeness" (Philippians 2:6, 7). In other words, Jesus, who is God, even humbled Himself and took on the lowly form of a human. If God can humble Himself, we certainly should be able to humble ourselves as well. And Scripture tells us He did this to become a servant. All believers need to combat pride by serving others. That's why Jesus washed His disciples' feet. He wanted to set an example for us. If the Son of God can serve others, so can we.

BENEFITS OF HUMILITY

Don't think humility is all lowness and drudgery. The benefits of humility far outweigh the (deceiving) benefits of pride. Philippians 2 describes how Jesus took on lowly, human form, and then it says, "Therefore God exalted him to the highest place and gave him the name that is above every name" (Philippians 2:9). When we stop exalting ourselves and accept a humble position, we make room for God to exalt us. And when God exalts us, it is true and lasting.

Furthermore, humility makes for a better quality of life, because it allows us to operate in the power of God, versus our own power. When we are prideful, we are relying on our own strength and goodness. But we cannot serve two masters (Matthew 6:24). We choose either to rely on our own strength, or on God's. Sometimes people are afraid to be humble. They think they will become a doormat, or others will walk all over them. Being humble doesn't mean being taken advantage of, but it does mean stepping out of the way and operating in the power of God, not your own. I love the image in Exodus 17 where the Amalekites come and attack the Israelites. Moses simply went to the top of the hill with the staff of God in his hands and stretched out his arms. Verse eleven says, "As long as Moses held up his hands, the Israelites were winning, but whenever he lowered his hands, the Amalekites were winning." But Aaron and Hur help Moses keep his hands up, and the Israelites defeated the Amalekites. I love that story. I picture Moses standing on the hill with his arms up, and to me it looks like an image of surrender. Surrendering is more about giving up than doing something. When we surrender to God, when we simply lift up our hands to Him, we give Him room to come in and fight our battles for us! Humility is a surrendered state that allows us to experience the power of God in our lives.

CONCLUSION

The Queen of Pride threatens to reign in all of our lives. As women, we may be tempted to be the best in something: beauty, talent, ability, knowledge, ministry, or family. We may be tempted to desire superiority. We may also be tempted to flaunt our strengths, particularly as a means of combating insecurity in another area. Or we may take self-esteem to unhealthy levels of vanity or arrogance. But as contrary as it seems to our human nature, it is always better to walk in humility rather than pride. As we walk in the Spirit, we can allow God to change our habits. Instead of being prideful, arrogant, and selfish, we can become humble servants who look out for the needs of others, not just ourselves. Put godly principles into place. Learn to apologize. Accept criticism. Let others have attention, or preferential treatment. Train yourself to perceive and tend to the well-being of others. Most importantly, surrender. Surrender your self-protection to God. Surrender your self-glorification to God. Rather than doing it yourself, give God room to be your Defender, to be the One who fights your battles, and the One who exalts you and honors you before others. This will only open your life up to the power of God, improve your relationships, and improve your livelihood. Most importantly, it improves your character to be more like Christ.

Prayer

Dear Holy Father,
You are God, by Yourself. There is no one like You, and no one beside. Lord, today I surrender my pride and give You Your rightful place in my

The Queen of Pride

life. Please forgive me for times when I was arrogant, when I negated correction, was boastful, or sought my own interests over the interests of others. God, I know what pride looks like, and I want to be like You. Give me a humble heart, and make me a true servant of both You and others. I surrender to You, and give You room to be my Defender. I will look to You for my validation, rather than glorify myself. I realize that my power is incredibly inferior to Yours, so today I choose to be humble before both You and others, and open my life to Your power. I ask these things in Jesus' Name. Amen.

Memory Verse

"Do nothing out of selfish ambition or vain conceit, but in humility consider others better than yourselves. Each of you should look not only to your own interests, but also to the interests of others."
PHILIPPIANS 2:3, 4

Reflection Questions

What makes you feel valuable? What sorts of things do you put your "stock" in?

How do you handle your successes, achievements, or virtues before other people?

Do you tend to shy away from attention or seek the spotlight?

How do you handle criticism? Are you defensive? Do you explain/justify yourself? Do you apologize?

Dethroning the Queen

Do you ever let others have the last word?

How aware are you of other people's actual needs, comfort, and interests? Do you tend to these things in others, or do you fend for yourself?

Are you comfortable serving others?

Are you comfortable humbling yourself? How does humility make you feel?

Are you willing to surrender your pride or selfishness and rely on God?

Action Plan!

This week, make it a point to find ways to look out for the concerns and well-being of others. Practice tending to these things before your own interests, and journal about your experience. Make sure you serve others in ways that they actually find helpful, instead of serving others in ways you think are best. (Sometimes in our desire to serve, we serve in ways that we think are good without stopping to make sure that the other person finds our actions beneficial. Serve according to what others think is best, not what you think is best.)

Also, if someone presents a concern or criticism to you, don't justify yourself first. Instead, listen first, and see if you need to apologize for anything.

CHAPTER THIRTEEN

Crowning the Princess

"But you are a chosen people, a royal priesthood, a holy nation,
a people belonging to God, that you may declare the praises of him
who called you out of darkness into his wonderful light."

1 PETER 2:9

HURRAY! We have reached the fun part of our journey: Crowning the Princess. This is a crucial step toward having a healthy relationship with God and each other as women. We don't just go through the pain of dethroning our fleshly ways; we experience the glory of being called a daughter of God! In order to tap into your full potential in the body of Christ, to be all you're called to be, to feel true self-worth, to experience the fullness of godly sisterhood, and to properly edify the body, you must let God dethrone the Queen Bee, and then crown the princess!

WHO WE ARE: LEGITIMATE HEIRS

Among His many names, God is called the King. David calls Him "the King of glory" (Psalms 24:7). He says, "Lift up your heads, O you gates; be lifted up, you ancient doors, that the King of glory may come in. Who is this King of glory? The Lord strong and mighty, the Lord mighty in battle... Who is he, this King of glory? The Lord Almighty—he is the King of glory" (Psalms 24:7–10). Paul also refers to God as, "The blessed and only Ruler, the King of kings and the Lord of lords" (1 Timothy 6:15). Of all the kings that ever walked this earth, and that ever will, God is the King of them all, the One who sits enthroned in heaven!

Dethroning the Queen

Now, Galatians 3:26 says, "You are all sons of God through faith in Christ Jesus," meaning that if we have accepted Christ, we are considered His children. First John 3:1a says, "How great is the love the Father has lavished on us, that we should be called children of God! And that is what we are!" Now think about that for a moment. If God is the King, and we are His children, then that means we are daughters of a King. And a daughter of a King is what? That's right—a princess! And we have become royalty, by God's grace, through Christ.

As princesses, we have great reason to rejoice. Romans 8:16, 17 says, "The Spirit himself testifies with our spirit that we are God's children. Now if we are children, then we are heirs—heirs of God and co-heirs with Christ." Galatians 3:29 says, "If you belong to Christ, then you are Abraham's seed, and heirs according to the promise." We are royalty with a great inheritance! We are heirs to God's exceeding great and precious promises.

Three Relationships

Now, our royalty affects three important relationships within the kingdom of God: our relationship to God, our relationship with other members of the body, and our "relationship" with ourselves. Let's quickly look at the implications of these relationships.

Our Relationship to God

Notice the relationship: King to princess, or Father to daughter. Through Christ we are royalty, yet we are still under authority. By accepting our identity as princesses, we are also accepting God's authority over us, and agreeing to live in total submission to Him.

Our Relationship to Others in the Body of Christ

If we are heirs, so are the people in the pew next to us. We ought to remember that all God's children, the mature and immature alike, are heirs with us, and we should treat them as such. Women, we should not roll

Crowning the Princess

our eyes at each other or despise each other. When we do, we are rolling our eyes at royalty. We should refrain, not because the children of God are so great and wonderful, but we refrain out of respect for God. To show love for people is to show love for God, and to show contempt for people is to show contempt for God. I know this is difficult. This is a rather challenging point for me. Sometimes I feel like saying, "God, I'm cool with you, but I don't know about all these other people running around here!" But we must remember we are only children of God by His grace, just like everyone else. We should show our appreciation, as well as reverence for God, by how we treat His other princes and princesses.

Our Relationship with Ourselves

Our relationship to God as our Father and King plays a huge role in how we view ourselves. It is so important for you to connect with your identity in Christ. This is critical for everyone, particularly for women. Here are three important points to embrace about yourself through your relationship with God:

1. The first truth about yourself to grasp we've already discussed a little: You are royalty. Believe it! Embrace it! We will discuss this in more detail in the next section, but really begin to receive this concept. Know that you are royalty! You are a princess! A true heir! There is so much dignity and worth in that fact. You are not a "nobody," you are not a pushover, you are not worthless—you are a daughter of God and He has called you royalty! Really reflect on that and begin to let it affect how you view yourself! The world may never give you your props, but that does not change who you truly are! If you are royalty, nothing can change that. That's why we are free to be humble servants, because no amount of demeaning labor, no harsh treatment, and no mean words can ever take our crowns!

Dethroning the Queen

2. The second truth to grasp is that you are fearfully and wonderfully made—a designer original! You are not a copy. God did not mass-produce humanity. You are not a clone of anybody else. Your creation did not begin in your mother's womb; your creation began in the mind of God. Psalms 139:13–16 says: "For you created my inmost being; you knit me together in my mother's womb. I will praise you because I am fearfully and wonderfully made; your works are wonderful; I know that full well. My frame was not hidden from you when I was made in the secret place. When I was woven together in the depths of the earth, your eyes saw my unformed body. All the days ordained for me were written in your book before one of them came to be."

   God made you by hand. The King himself went to his secret place to conceive you in His mind, then like a genius working in the depths He wove you together, bringing together your unique combination of personal characteristics. He stamped you with His image, and made you in His own likeness, for you were made to reflect His glory. And when He was finished, He looked over his creation and smiled. And then He declared that you are wonderful! Praise be to God for the glory of His creation in you!

3. Finally, know that you are unconditionally loved! All of us want to be loved, right? God loves you so incredibly much that you cannot possibly comprehend it! I love the way God puts it in Isaiah 54:10: "Though the mountains be shaken and the hills be removed, yet my unfailing love for you will not be shaken." God's love for you cannot be shaken. His love for you is stronger than the foundations of the earth. God's love gives you innate value. First John 4:7–21 tells us that God is love. He loves us perfectly, for the very essence of His nature is perfect

love. You have done nothing to earn His love, thus you can do nothing to lose His love. God's love for you is fixed, constant, and unchanging. He loves you because it is the essence of Him to love you. You are of great worth and value in His sight.

WEARING THE CROWN

We have a responsibility to conduct ourselves according to our value. The world will threaten and challenge us, but it's our job to keep a level head about ourselves and not let our self-esteem and sense of self be shaken.

That said, you are a princess. You have got to walk, talk, act, speak, sit, and stand like the princess you are! People wonder why I wear heels all the time, and it's because I know who I am! The clothes don't make me, but when I get dressed up, I feel affirmed in my identity as royalty. It's not that I need my clothes to dictate who I am, but I want to dress like who I really am. It encourages a healthy mentality—reminding me I am valuable and loved.

Not only do you have to know who you are for you, but you must be who you are before others. When you face Queen Bees, or anyone who would tear you down and speak against who you are, gracefully refuse to let them affect you negatively. You are a daughter of God, a princess. Also, because you are a princess, you don't have to look down on anybody to make yourself feel good. You already have an overflowing well of validation that comes from God, not man. The princess method to validation is far superior to the Queen Bee method, and it's also more godly.

Now being a princess, again, doesn't mean walking around with your nose in the air. That would be a Queen Bee, needing to act prideful, vain, or arrogant to feel good about herself. You are a true princess, and that never changes. Therefore, you are free to serve in humility, because you know ultimately God will honor you in the end. And since you are a princess in the kingdom of God, you should be a true reflection of your King. That means showing the fruits of the Spirit, "Love, joy, peace, patience, kindness, goodness, faithfulness, gentleness, and self-control" (Galatians 5:22, 23). These are the attributes of a princess in the kingdom of God. We are not stuck-up royalty, like Queen Bees, who really aren't acting anything like royalty at all. Queen Bee characteristics are of the flesh, not representing the kingdom of God, but the kingdom of the Devil! Galatians 5:19–21a says, "The acts of the sinful nature are obvious...hatred, discord, jealousy, fits of rage, selfish ambition, dissentions, factions, and envy." Too many women act in these ways, like Queen Bees. But a true princess relinquishes these and exhibits the fruit of the Spirit, being a true reflection of her Father in heaven.

Finishing it Off

I encourage you to let the Holy Spirit perfect God's will in you by dethroning the Queen Bee and crowning the princess. You will have a healthier view of yourself and others when you do. One thing that is critical to that process is embracing brokenness. Being dethroned really hurts—really. I remember when the Lord dealt with me about my jealousy toward one of my friends. It was excruciating to confront. God had me humble myself, not just before Him, but before my friend as well. I came before her weeping and confessed that I had been jealous and resentful, and that it was getting in the way of our friendship. It was painful, but at the same time, it was so freeing and liberating. Through the brokenness, a heavy burden lifted off of me. My friend and I had a good heart to heart and discussed some things that had been under the surface for a long time. And what's more, she forgave me for my jealousy, and that really opened the gates for a much better friendship. Brokenness hurts, but God wants to put the pieces back together to form a much more beautiful picture.

Also, please don't try to dethrone the Queen in your own strength. Rely on the power of the Holy Spirit to transform and change you. It is truly a work that only He can do. As He leads, simply obey and do your end. But it is by the Spirit that we bear good fruit and put the flesh to death. Galatians 5:16 says, "So I say, live by the Spirit, and you will not gratify the desires of the sinful nature." I am not saying you don't have a part to play, for it is your job to surrender, let your mind be renewed, and be obedient according to God's will. But it starts with living by the Spirit. Jesus says, "I am the vine, you are the branches. If a man remains in me and I in him, he will bear much fruit; apart from me you can do nothing" (John 15:5). Walk in the Spirit, and as you put to death the sinful nature of the Queen Bee, God will manifest a true princess in you!

Prayer

Perhaps you are a woman who knows God, and are taking a step toward becoming more like Him by allowing Him to remove the qualities of the flesh and replace them with qualities of the Spirit. But perhaps you are reading this book, and you have not yet entered into His family. God loves you, and He wants nothing more than to invite you in, to call you His daughter and make you an heir to all of His wonderful promises, including salvation and everlasting life. He says He stands at the door and knocks, and to anyone who hears Him and opens the door, He will come in (Revelation 3:20). If that is you, then I invite you to pray this prayer:

Dear God,
Thank You for loving me and for knowing me before the world began. I look to You, God, to fill the void in my life. I want to be a part of Your family, to experience Your love and all the wonderful blessings that come with being a child of God. So today, I ask You to come into my heart. I ask forgiveness for my old ways, and turn now to Your ways. I confess with my mouth and believe in my heart that Jesus is Lord, and that through him, Your Son, You came to the earth in human form, and died on the cross for my sins. I believe that Jesus rose from the dead, and that through Him I have victory, salvation, and eternal life. Thank You for bringing me into Your family! In Jesus' Name, I pray. Amen!

Dethroning the Queen

Now, as we close, let's all pray for God to help us become the women we were called and destined to be!

Dear God, my King,
Thank You so much for Your life-giving Word that corrects, instructs, shapes, and guides me. Thank You for Your gracious promises, for salvation, and for calling me Your child. I know I am a princess, and an heir to Your promises, so I commit to walking upright according to my calling. Holy Spirit I ask You now to do the work that only You can do. Reshape me. Dethrone my sinful, Queen Bee nature. Improve my attitude toward women, and improve my relationships with women. Create in me a clean heart, one that is humble, pure, and truly beautiful. Make me a true reflection of You, a princess who represents Your kingdom and bears the fruit of Your Spirit. Help me to truly embrace my identity in You, and let it overflow in my relationship with You and with others. And I give You all the thanks and praise for who You are, and how You are going to transform my life and my relationships! I pray these things in Jesus' Name. Amen!"

Memory Verses

"But you are a chosen people, a royal priesthood, a holy nation, a people belonging to God, that you may declare the praises of him who called you out of darkness into his wonderful light."
1 PETER 2:9

"I praise you because I am fearfully and wonderfully made; your works are wonderful, I know that full well."
PSALMS 139:14

"Though the mountains be shaken and the hills be removed, yet my unfailing love for you will not be shaken."
ISAIAH 54:10

Crowning the Princess

Reflection Questions

How does a Queen Bee compare to a princess? Which is healthier? Which is more beneficial?

What does it mean to be a princess? How does that make you feel? Are you able to embrace that?

What are three ways you can be less like a Queen Bee and more like a princess?

How would you treat a princess? How would you treat a king? Does your treatment of other people coincide with the fact that other believers are children of God?

If one description of God is "the King of glory," how can that be reflected in your treatment of Him? How can that be reflected in your praise and worship?

Since God calls us His little girls, what does that mean for how we can relate to and approach God?

Action Plan!

Do something for yourself today that affirms you are a princess! Also, start letting your prayer, praise, and worship reflect the fact that you are a princess speaking to the King.

Notes

Chapter 1:

1. *Mean Girls,* Directed by Mark Waters, Paramount Pictures, M.G. Films, Broadway Video, 2004.

Chapter 3:

1. *America's Next Top Model,* Directed by Claudia Frank, 10 by 10 Entertainment, Pottle Productions, Ty Ty Baby Productions, (2003–2007).

Chapter 4:

1. *The New International Webster's Concise Dictionary of the English Language,* 2002 ed., s.v. "Compete."

Chapter 5:

1. *The New International Webster's Concise Dictionary of the English Language,* 2002 ed., s.v. "Jealous."
2. *The New International Webster's Concise Dictionary of the English Language,* 2002 ed., s.v. "Envy."

Chapter 7:

1. *The New International Webster's Concise Dictionary of the English Language,* 2002 ed., s.v. "Reconcile."

Chapter 8:

1. *The New International Webster's Concise Dictionary of the English Language,* 2002 ed., s.v. "Judge."
2. *The Lord of the Rings: The Fellowship of the Ring,* Directed by Peter Jackson, New Line Cinema, WingNut Films, 2001.

Chapter 9:

1. *Mean Girls,* Directed by Mark Waters, Paramount Pictures, M.G. Films, Broadway Video, 2004.

Dethroning the Queen

Chapter 10:

1. *The New International Webster's Concise Dictionary of the English Language,* 2002 ed., s.v. "Slander."
2. *The New International Webster's Concise Dictionary of the English Language,* 2002 ed., s.v. "Gossip."
3. *The New International Webster's Concise Dictionary of the English Language,* 2002 ed., s.v. "Discreet."

Chapter 11:

1. *Mean Girls,* Directed by Mark Waters, Paramount Pictures, M.G. Films, Broadway Video, 2004.
2. *The New International Webster's Concise Dictionary of the English Language,* 2002 ed., s.v. "Witchcraft."
3. *The New International Webster's Concise Dictionary of the English Language,* 2002 ed., s.v. "Magic."

Chapter 12:

1. *The New International Webster's Concise Dictionary of the English Language,* 2002 ed., s.v. "Humble."

Bibliography

America's Next Top Model. Directed by Claudia Frank. 10 by 10 Entertainment, Pottle Productions, Ty Ty Baby Productions, 2003–2007.

Mean Girls. Directed by Mark Waters. Paramount Pictures, M.G. Films, Broadway Video, 2004.

The Lord of the Rings: The Fellowship of the Ring. Directed by Peter Jackson. New Line Cinema, WingNut Films, 2001.